Take Pain Control
Into Your Own Hands

"Whoever is spared personal pain must feel himself called to help in diminishing the pain of others. We must all carry our share of the misery which lies upon the world."

- Albert Schweitzer, physician, philosopher, Nobel Peace Prize Laureate

Take Pain Control Into Your Own Hands

Rapid and Dramatic Pain Relief
With Korean Hand Therapy
Self Treatment

Ilana Newman, MD

Newman Medical Enterprises, Inc.
NewmanMedicalEnterprises.com
Pembroke Pines, FL

Photograph on page 304 © The Wu Project, Inc.
All other illustrations and images, including the TPC Hand Logo © Newman Medical Enterprise, Inc.
Photographs by Arik Levy.
Cover design by Pixelstudio.

Paperback ISBN: 978-0-9967508-9-9
Library of Congress Control Number 2018901437

First Edition
February 2018

Dedicated to everyone who has taken me up on an offer to use Korean Hand Therapy to relieve their pain. Without your willingness to let me help you, I would never have discovered how effective this system is.

Special thanks to my husband and son, for their endless patience during the creation of this book.

Legal Disclaimer

This book is for educational and informational purposes only and the content is not intended to be a substitute for professional medical advice, diagnosis, or treatment. Always seek the advice of your physician or other qualified health provider with any questions you may have regarding any medical condition you have. If you think you may be suffering from any medical condition, you should seek immediate medical attention.

You should never delay seeking medical advice, disregard medical advice, or discontinue medical treatment because of information in this book. You must not rely on the information in this book as an alternative to medical advice from your doctor or other professional healthcare provider.

The information presented here is for self treatment of pain. In most parts of the world, there are legal restrictions against any kind of touch therapies performed by people without professional licenses. If you are licensed in a profession that is allowed to touch people (such as a doctor, nurse, physical therapist, massage therapist, chiropractor, or acupuncturist), Correspondence Korean Hand Therapy may be within your scope of practice.

"It is easier to find men who will volunteer to die, than to find those who are willing to endure pain with patience."

- Julius Caesar

Table of Contents

"Illness is the doctor to whom we pay most heed; to kindness, to knowledge, we make promise only; pain we obey."

- Marcel Proust

Limitations of This System

Un-investigated pain needs to be approached cautiously. Any pain treatment modality that can temporarily reduce pain, including over-the-counter and prescription pain medications, could cause long-term harm by masking life-threatening conditions that are not detected and treated in time. Use of Correspondence Korean Hand Therapy in such situations may help with pain but could further delay seeking medical evaluation and treatment.

Important Considerations:

- Do not use this system to treat severe abdominal pain if there is the possibility that you might have appendicitis. Delayed treatment of appendicitis may lead to rupture of the appendix, septic shock, or death.

- Do not use this system to treat severe abdominal pain if there is a possibility that you may be pregnant. Symptoms of ectopic pregnancy can be non-specific and treatment is often delayed, risking tubal rupture, heavy bleeding into the abdomen, or death.

- Do not use this system to treat severe headaches or neurological symptoms that may be due to life-threatening brain conditions, such as cerebral hemorrhage or stroke. Symptoms such as slurred speech or facial droop, or severe headaches that wake people from sleep or are associated with uncontrolled vomiting, require immediate medical attention.

- Do not use this system if you are pregnant without first consulting an acupuncturist familiar with Korean Hand Therapy. There are body acupuncture points that must be avoided during pregnancy because they might cause uterine contractions or premature labor. Because of this, I feel that the analogous points in Korean Hand Therapy also should be avoided during pregnancy. There are acupuncturists who are trained to do acupuncture during pregnancy, but as a medical doctor, I take a more conservative approach and do not use acupuncture in anyone who is pregnant or may be pregnant.

- Do not treat dental pain with this system as a way to avoid seeing a dentist when you have a dental problem. Delayed treatment of a cavity can lead to an abscess or could require a root canal. I only use Korean Hand Therapy to treat dental pain when someone is already under the care of a dentist or after they schedule an appointment. Korean Hand Therapy can be a big help in easing dental pain while you are waiting for the problem to be fixed by the dentist.

- Pain from anatomical injuries that won't heal without surgery, such as misaligned broken bones or torn ligaments, can be treated with Korean Hand Therapy but the results will be less dramatic than with other types of pain. Korean Hand Therapy can offer symptomatic relief but it will not replace the need for surgical repair.

- Nerve damage in the hands can make treating pain with Korean Hand Therapy less effective. If only one hand has nerve damage, the opposite hand should be used for better results.

- Neuropathic pain in the body is especially difficult to treat, even with Western medical approaches. When nerves are the source of the pain, a system that uses signals along nerve pathways to treat pain may not work. Korean Hand Therapy may help, but the pain relief will likely be less profound than with other types of pain.

Once your pain has been evaluated by a doctor or if you are sure that the underlying cause of your pain is not a dangerous one, Correspondence Korean Hand Therapy will be a useful tool to reduce your pain level. It can be used in combination with or in place of over-the-counter and prescription pain medications, physical therapy, acupuncture or other treatment modalities. It also can help with post-operative pain if surgical treatment is required.

"It is not death or pain that is to be dreaded,
but the fear of pain or death."

- Epictetus

How to Use This Book

This book focuses on practical applications of Correspondence Korean Hand Therapy for self-treatment of pain. After several years of using and teaching this system, I have simplified the method so that anyone can learn and use it. Recognizing the landmarks on the hands that represent corresponding body areas is no more difficult than reading a map. Locating the discrete painful points on your hands to treat your own pain is easy.

I thought it would be best to begin by giving you my recommendation on how to approach reading this book. My suggestion is to immediately skip to page 51 and start learning about the map of the body on your hands. Don't bother getting bogged down with the details about my acupuncture training, how I came to learn about Korean Hand Therapy, theories on how it may work, or a review of some of the research documenting its effectiveness. Those are all important but none of them will make it any easier for you to learn how to do this yourself. And, to be honest, they may distract you from diving directly into learning the technique. All this information is included in the book for you to review at your leisure if you become impressed by your results with Korean Hand Therapy and want to learn more about this amazing system. I considered moving the first chapters to the end of the book so you would go straight to the practical information, but that is not how books are typically structured.

At the end of this book, there are two chapters with exercises that will help you integrate the information presented in the earlier chapters. You will draw the map of the body on the hands on blank hand drawings, marking the landmarks that help you locate the areas on your hands to treat pain in your body. Then, you will have the opportunity to quiz yourself by looking at photographs of different points on the hands and identifying the corresponding body areas. I encourage you to take advantage of these training tools to deepen your understanding of Correspondence Korean Hand Therapy. The more familiar you become with this system, the more likely you will be to use it and benefit from it.

If you have questions or comments about this book or Korean Hand Therapy, please go to TakePainControl.com to submit them. I will answer questions during monthly webinars that will start in March 2018 and you can watch the replays if you cannot participate live.

Why I Wrote This Book

A Bit About Me

Twenty years ago as a family medicine resident, I was surprised by how many of my patients had chronic back pain. Many of them came to the clinic with long stories of all the things they had tried to remedy their pain, including applications of heat or ice, over-the-counter medications and physical therapy sessions. Some brought copies of their radiology films and reports, which were often normal or showed mild degenerative changes. Rarely did these patients have any documented anatomical abnormalities that required surgery or put them at risk of spinal cord injuries.

During residency training, we were taught that the standard next step for these patients was to start opioid pain medications. The importance of treating chronic pain was heavily emphasized at that time, and pain was hailed as the "fifth vital sign" (after temperature, blood pressure, heart rate, and respiratory rate). The new long-acting opioid Oxycontin was approved during my first year of residency. Pharmaceutical companies were spending large sums of money on medical education programs for physicians about treating pain. We were bombarded with information from reputable sources telling us these medications were safe, the extended-release formulations reduced the risk of addiction, and that physicians were ethically obligated to aggressively treat chronic pain with opioids. However, this approach did not make sense to me because I knew the patients would need to keep taking opioid medications forever, with increasing doses required as they became tolerant to them over time.

My family medicine residency program had several physicians who integrated acupuncture and other complementary medicine modalities into their medical practices. I was granted permission to use my elective rotation time to study acupuncture in a program for physicians through the University of California in Los Angeles. The program required attendance at a live introductory session, several months of home study, and another ten days of live practice sessions to review acupuncture point locations and needling techniques. The course fulfilled the New York State requirement of 300 hours of training in order for physicians to do acupuncture.

The acupuncture course included a small section on ear acupuncture. I thought the idea of treating the whole body with just the ear was interesting, but at the time I was focused on mastering the complicated theories of body acupuncture. Learning acupuncture is especially difficult for medical doctors, as our minds have already been molded to think of symptoms and causes of health problems in the context of allopathic medicine. I am sure it is easier for acupuncturists who enroll in Oriental Medical School without these preconceived ideas. Unlike Western medicine, which focuses on fixing problems after they occur, acupuncture targets the underlying imbalances that predispose patients to develop their problems. This approach of treating problems at the root is why several sessions of acupuncture may be required before improvement is noted and why it is common for people to stop acupuncture treatments before they have given it a chance. In our modern society, many people are impatient and prefer a quick fix to a more comprehensive solution.

My acupuncture training was in French-style acupuncture. It is significantly different from what is taught in most Oriental Medical schools and is based on the first translations of the ancient acupuncture texts by French Jesuit priests in China. This approach emphasizes the importance of figuring out a person's biopsychosocial type to select the best treatment. It also uses unique needling techniques to release the blockages that cause symptoms and disease. Two people with the same complaints would get acupuncture treatment using different points, because the point selection takes into account their individual personalities, physiologies, and underlying imbalances that led them to develop problems.

During my adolescent medicine fellowship, I enrolled in the NADA (National Acupuncture Detox Association) ear acupuncture detoxification training. The program was two weeks long and took place at Lincoln Hospital in the Bronx, NY. The NADA program started as a grassroots effort to find a solution to the heroin addiction problem in New York City in the 1970s. The NADA protocol uses five short acupuncture needles in each ear that are left in place for 45 minutes. The treatment is so effective that people sentenced to a drug detoxification program through the New York court system can choose between ear acupuncture or methadone treatment because urine drug screen tests show they work equally well. There is even a special license in New York, allowing inpatient drug program staff who have completed the NADA training to insert addiction protocol needles into clients' ears, under the supervision of an acupuncturist or a medical doctor licensed to perform acupuncture.

Ear acupuncture is also a powerful modality for treating pain anywhere on the body. Using the map of the body on the ear developed by Dr. Paul Nogier in the 1950s, the appropriate points are stimulated by inserting needles, acupressure with manual stimulation, beads or seeds taped to the ear, electrical stimulation, or laser treatments. Not only does ear acupuncture eliminate the need to select several acupuncture points from the body meridians to compose an effective treatment, but the pain-relieving results of ear acupuncture are more rapid than with body acupuncture.

Another advantage of ear acupuncture over body acupuncture is that the ear provides information on what points need to be treated, by changes in color or texture of the ear, tenderness when pressure is applied to specific locations, or increased electrical conduction/decreased resistance that is detected with a point location device. Ear acupuncture does not require patients to disrobe or lay face down for treatment, which makes it a great choice for many patients. It also allows ear acupuncture treatments to be done in group settings, with patients seated in chairs. I proposed doing a research study of ear acupuncture for smoking cessation in teenagers during my adolescent medicine fellowship, but was told by the hospital administration that they did not allow anyone to do acupuncture.

After moving to Florida, I learned about another acupuncture course for physicians at the University of Miami and I completed their basic and advanced training programs. This was about 10 years after I did my first acupuncture training and it was a good review and an opportunity to learn a more Traditional Chinese Medicine style of acupuncture. My acupuncture teachers at the University of Miami were Chinese medical doctors who had earned their MD degrees in China while also studying Traditional Chinese Medicine. It was also the first time I learned about scalp acupuncture, which is an acupuncture microsystem used primarily for neurological problems.

The ear acupuncture sections at the University of Miami programs were taught by Dr. Tom Corbin, who was a physician assistant before going to Oriental Medical School and studying in China. He was the acupuncturist at a local Veteran's Hospital, where the medical doctors referred their most complicated pain cases to him after they ran out of treatment options. During his ear acupuncture seminars, I rediscovered my love of ear acupuncture. My patients were impressed with the speed of their pain relief when I treated their ears and many preferred getting treatments without needles. It became the primary acupuncture modality I used, with a few important body acupuncture points occasionaly added.

A few years after completing the acupuncture courses, I did a fellowship in Hospice and Palliative Medicine at the University of Miami. I was the only medical doctor with acupuncture privileges at the hospital and used acupuncture to help several patients with complicated pain problems. I helped out with the University of Miami acupuncture course by volunteering during the practice sessions.

After finishing my fellowship, I began co-teaching the ear acupuncture course with Dr. Corbin. Because the ear acupuncture modules can be taken separately from the full acupuncture course, several of the attendees each year are medical doctors with no prior acupuncture training. Some of them are so impressed with the pain relief their patients get with treating just the ear, they later enroll in the full acupuncture course. Dr. Corbin and I also attended a conference in 2014 at Johns Hopkins University, with auriculotherapy lectures by experts from around the world and a mix of acupuncturist and medical doctor attendees.

How Korean Hand Therapy Found Me

I learned about Korean Hand Therapy by accident, but life is full of unexpected events that lead us in fortuitous directions. I wanted an extra copy of the textbook from my UCLA acupuncture course because I sometimes lend mine to acupuncturist friends who are curious about the different approach I had learned. I found one on eBay and it came with another book - Koryo Hand Acupuncture by Dr. Tae Woo Yoo. After the books arrived, I flipped through Koryo Hand Acupuncture and noticed the similarity to ear acupuncture, but set the book aside and almost forgot about it. Years later, I received an email from Dr. Dan Lobash with dates of his Korean Hand Therapy seminars in Miami. I remembered the Koryo Hand Acupuncture book and was surprised to find out that Dr. Lobash learned Korean Hand Therapy from Dr. Yoo when he came to the United States many years earlier. An acupuncturist friend came with me to Dr. Lobash's training. and thus my introduction to Korean Hand Therapy began. I later took Dr. Lobash's advanced training and have recommend his seminars to acupuncturists and friends. He now has online seminars that are accredited for continuing education credits for acupuncturists.

A couple of years later, I searched online for more books by Dr. Yoo. Although Dr. Yoo has published many books in Korean and Japanese, only a fraction of them have been translated into English and they are difficult to find. I found a Korean acupuncturist in England, Dr. Jong Baik, who teaches Korean Hand Therapy and sells Korean Hand Therapy supplies throughout Europe. I purchased a few copies of Dr. Yoo's small book about the Golden Meridian, also known as the Ren or Conception Vessel Meridian, that runs down the center of the front of the body and the hand.

After receiving my order, Dr. Baik's wife, Nataly, emailed me and suggested that I travel to Darlington, England for one of Dr. Baik's seminars. The United Kingdom seemed too far away, so I politely declined. Dr. Baik's wife emailed me again, when someone paid the deposit for an upcoming Korean Hand Therapy seminar but could not attend. They offered me the spot in the class at a reduced rate and I was able to get time off work for the trip. Since then, I have traveled to England several times to take Dr. Baik's Korean Hand Therapy courses, including his annual Master Class. I also had the privilege of shadowing him on some of his clinic days at the local hospice. His experience in using Korean Hand Therapy to manage symptoms in cancer patients has benefited several of my palliative medicine patients with pain, hot flashes, and nausea.

Advantages of Korean Hand Therapy Over Other Microsystems

I am a big fan of ear acupuncture and have been a co-instructor of the ear acupuncture modules at the University of Miami's acupuncture course for physicians for several years. Despite all my experience, I find treating myself using the ear very difficult, if not impossible. Even with the use of mirrors, it is impossible for me to comfortably insert needles into my own ears at the precise locations needed. I have used electrical point finders and stimulators on my own ear, but I cannot tell what points were detected and treated. Unlike with ears, our hands are always accessible for close inspection and self-treatment. And while foot re-flexology feels good, it is almost never acceptable for people to take off their shoes and rub their feet in public!

One of the biggest reasons I have such a deep passion for Correspondence Korean Hand Therapy, is that it can be done anywhere, at any time, and with no special tools needed. It can be done while sitting, talking on the phone, lying down, or walking around. It can be comfortably used on young children, the elderly, and needle-phobic people. It is truly the best kept secret in pain management.

Anyone Can Learn How to
Take Pain Control Into Your Own Hands

This system is so simple that even my son learned which fingers represent the arms, legs, and head just by watching me treat his teachers when he was four years old. If Corre-spondence Korean Hand Therapy was taught in elementa-ry schools, the impact on pain around the world would be staggering.

If you can point to the location of the pain in your body, there is a corresponding area on the hands that can treat it. If you can read a map, you can locate the points on your hands that correspond to any part of your body. If you can write your name, you can effectively stimulate the points on your hands to relieve your pain.

At many of my workshops, attendees have asked if there was a book they can buy with the information I presented to share with friends and family who would benefit from learning how to treat their own pain. I tell them about Dr. Yoo's textbooks but explain that they are difficult to find in bookstores and the Correspondence Therapy section is only a small section out of hundreds of pages that primarily focus on acupuncture concepts. Some students have suggested that I create a book version of my workshop and that is what I have done here.

I hope you find this book interesting but, more importantly, I hope you become curious enough to use this technique to treat your own pain. Even if you cannot imagine that something so easy could work, I urge you to suspend your skepticism long enough to try it. Unlike most other treatments for pain, there are no potential side effects of Correspondence Korean Hand Therapy, other than maybe a little discomfort on your hands from poking on them. However, the risk of missing out on a way to quickly reduce your pain and improve your quality of life is significant.

You do not need to be a healthcare professional to treat your own pain. You do not need to have any knowledge of acupuncture meridians or Traditional Chinese Medicine theory. And you do not have to memorize complicated hand or foot reflexology maps with the body locations scattered in random patterns.

The biggest problem I have seen with people who have learned Correspondence Korean Hand Therapy to treat their own pain is that they forget to use it. Hopefully, this book will serve as a reminder to think about your hands whenever you find that you are in pain.

"All pain is one malady with many names."

- Antiphanes

Pain Needs to Be Treated

Pain Is a Big Problem

Pain is one of the most poorly understood medical conditions. It a symptom with many causes and cannot be objectively detected or measured. Much of the current medical research on pain focuses on how the brain perceives pain and how pain medications or other interventions work. There are many proposed theories but the exact mechanisms are still unknown.

Everyone experiences pain during their life. I often tell my patients that no one really has a pain score of zero out of ten, because being alive hurts a little. If you stop and think about it, there is always a little discomfort in our backs or feet from normal activities.

Acute pain usually resolves when the underlying cause improves. Pain that continues for three to six months is chronic and can have long-term, negative effects on multiple aspects of life, such as sleep, mood, work, and relationships with others. Chronic pain limits normal range of motion and the ability to continue normal activities, which leads to further decreases in function and increased pain.

The Institute of Medicine of the National Academies estimates 100 million Americans are living with chronic pain.

Pain negatively affects quality of life and it also has a significant economic impact, both personal and as a society. Low back pain is the most common reason for job-related disability and is a common reason for missed work and decreased job productivity, along with headaches. The economic cost associated with chronic pain in the United States is estimated to be between 560 and 635 billion dollars each year.

People with pain refuse to take medication for various reasons. Some prefer to wait and see if the pain will disappear (although most of them will admit this tactic has never worked for them in the past). Others view not tolerating pain as a sign of weakness, they do not want to become dependent on medication, or they fear the side effects of medications more than the negative effect of untreated pain on their lives.

Delaying pain treatment until it becomes unbearable is not a good strategy. When pain is severe, oral pain medications will not work fast enough because it can take up to 30 minutes for them to be absorbed. Pain medication taken too late will be less effective as the same dose would have been if taken earlier, when the pain was less intense. Even with acute pain that is expected to be temporary, such as a minor injury or a headache, avoiding treatment prolongs suffering and reduces normal function.

The Opioid Crisis

The United States is in the midst of an opioid crisis. According to the National Center for Health Statistics, there were an average of 46 overdose deaths each day involving prescription opioid medications in 2016. Because of widespread misuse and abuse of prescription medications, many states have limited the amount of opioids that pharmacies can dispense - even to patients who truly need them. Pharmacies maintain smaller stocks of opioids, to reduce their involvement in inappropriate dispensing of these medications and to deter thieves from stealing them. Many emergency rooms and urgent care centers are implementing "no opioid" policies to discourage drug-seeking patients from seeking care at their facilities.

As a medical doctor, I am licensed to prescribe opioid medications if a patient needs them. As a palliative medicine doctor who specializes in treating pain and other difficult to manage symptoms in patients with life-limiting conditions, often prescribe opioids at higher than typical doses. While opioid medications offer temporary relief, the side effects of sedation, nausea, and severe constipation can negatively affect quality of life.

The stigma of opioids has also affected the cancer patients I have treated. Many are reluctant to take their pain medications due to fears of becoming addicted to them or experiencing harsh side effects. Some patients are also afraid of being unable to refill their prescriptions if opioids become harder to get and admit to taking fewer doses than

what is prescribed to make sure they do not run out before
they are able to refill them.

Do Not Ignore Your Pain

I support the idea of not taking pain medications unnec-
essarily, but the alternative plan cannot be to do nothing and just suffer through it. Pain is a signal from your
body that needs to be acknowledged. Over-the-counter
pain medications can be useful and their risks can be min-
imized if taken as directed and used as briefly as possible.
There are multiple non-drug modalities that can be help
make pain bearable so that people can continue activities
important to them. Correspondence Korean Hand Therapy
is a great option for anyone with acute or chronic pain. Not
only does it offer a safe and effective way to manage pain,
it also encourages people to take an active role in helping
themselves.

What Is Korean Hand Therapy?

I'm sure you have several questions about Korean Hand Therapy. I thought it would be best to answer the questions I am most often asked when I tell people that I use a technique to manage pain by poking on the hands.

What Is Korean Hand Therapy?

In Korean, Korean Hand Therapy is called Koryo Sooji Chim, meaning "Korean Hand Acupuncture." Seo Geum or Seo Keum are other common names for it. The name also is frequently abbreviated as "KHT."

Korean Hand Therapy is considered an acupuncture microsystem, where the entire body is projected onto a small part. Acupuncture microsystems are an accessory way to do acupuncture treatments, similar to how a computer mouse is a secondary way to access and affect the information on a computer. The foundation of Korean Hand Therapy is Correspondence Theory, with the entire body represented on each hand. There are many known acupuncture microsystems with the entire body mapped onto a smaller part of the body and the most well known ones are the ear and scalp acupuncture microsystems.

Unlike most other acupuncture microsystems, Korean Hand Therapy is a complete microsystem with all the Traditional Chinese Medicine meridian pathways represented on the hands as well. Because of this, any acupuncture treatment protocol can be easily replicated on the hands using Basic Korean Hand Therapy. Korean Hand Therapy is safer than body acupuncture because, when using the hand, the risk of accidentally inserting needles into organs and blood vessels or causing a pneumothorax (collapsed lung) are eliminated.

Advanced Korean Hand Therapy involves more complicated acupuncture theories, including Five Elements and Eight Extraordinary Meridians. There are some treatment approaches that are unique to Korean Hand Therapy, including Three Constitutions (where a diagnosis is made by comparing qualities of the carotid and radial pulses with abdominal palpation) and Ring Therapy (where each of the five fingers represents one of the Five Elements, with gold or silver rings used to offset imbalances.) Dr. Yoo continues to refine and update his Korean Hand Therapy system. Currently there are 14 meridians and 404 distinct points identified on the hand in Korean Hand Therapy.

Korean Hand Therapy often involves the use of hand needles, which are shorter than ear or body acupuncture needles. Because the skin on the hands is thicker than other parts of the body, Korean Hand Therapy needles require the use of insertion tools to get them into the skin. In Korea and Japan, needles and moxa are commonly used in Korean Hand Therapy. In Western culture, these are not appealing to most people, so pressure with blunt probes or press pellets are preferred.

Korean Hand Therapy is widely accepted and used in South Korea. In 1994, the South Korean Supreme Court ruled to allow anyone to use needles to treat others with Korean Hand Therapy as long it is done without charge. Even in the United States, some of my Korean patients use Korean Hand Therapy to treat each other at church groups. In one patient with cancer, I used press pellets in addition to prescription medications for severe nausea while she was hospitalized. The patient's daughter, who grew up in the United States, was a bit shocked when I told her what I was doing. She said that the older generation believes in "that kind of stuff," but she didn't think it worked and was surprised when I told her it did.

A big advantage of Korean Hand Therapy over other acupuncture microsystems is that treatments can be continued at home. Results are better and last longer when interventions do not require an office visit. Self-treatment with Korean Hand Therapy can be done at any place and at any time.

How Was Korean Hand Therapy Discovered?

Tae Woo Yoo, OMD, PhD, a South Korean acupuncturist, discovered, developed and researched Korean Hand Therapy. In 1971, Dr. Yoo had a headache that would not go away. He tried to sleep but awoke with the idea that the tip of the middle finger represented the head. With a ballpoint pen, he poked on the area of the finger that he believed corresponded to the area where the headache was located and noted the area was sensitive to pressure. He then inserted an acupuncture needle into the tender point on his middle finger and his headache went away within minutes. Even as an experienced acupuncturist, he was amazed at the speed and degree of pain relief.

Between 1971 and 1975, Dr. Yoo studied and refined his theory of Korean Hand Therapy. In addition to identifying the map of the body on the hands, Dr. Yoo located all the acupuncture meridians on each hand and developed unique treatment theories. To confirm his findings, thermographic photography was used to measure changes in temperature. This was a state-of-the-art technology back in the 1970s, long before the recent development of functional MRI scans now used to study the effects of acupuncture in the brain. Dr. Yoo showed that significant temperature changes occur in various parts of the body after stimulation of corresponding parts on the hands, proving that treating the hands has profound systemic effects.

Dr. Yoo has continued to refine his system over the years. The main textbook, Koryo Hand Acupuncture, was first published in English in 1988 and the third edition, retitled Koryo Hand Therapy, was published in 2011. There are over 70 supplemental books that have been published in multiple languages, but only a few have been translated into English.

Korean Hand Therapy research continues to be done and published. Every two years, there is a large conference in South Korea, where research on Korean Hand Therapy is presented in Korean and Japanese to thousands of attendees. At the 2014 conference, Dr. Jong Baik, gave a presentation about the benefits of Korean Hand Therapy as a preventative treatment and shared some of his students' clinical experiences.

Why Are There Different Hand Maps?

If you do an online search for "Korean Hand Therapy," the results might be confusing. There are several online images of maps of the body on the hand, some with conflicting locations of key areas of the body. One of the alternative versions is Su Jok ("Hand Foot") Therapy, created by Dr. Park Jae Woo in South Korea in the late 1980s after he learned Dr. Tae Woo Yoo's Korean Hand Therapy. Su Jok differs most strikingly from Korean Hand Therapy by the location of the head on the thumb, with the arms on the index and pinky fingers and the legs on the middle and ring fingers.

Su Jok Therapy is better known in Russia and India while Korean Hand Therapy is better known in South Korea and Japan. Dr. Yoo has adamantly stated that Korean Hand Therapy is more effective and warned that some Su Jok protocols can be dangerous.

What Is Correspondence
Korean Hand Therapy?

Correspondence Theory is the most basic form of Korean Hand Therapy. It comprises only 21 pages of the first edition of Dr. Yoo's 473 page textbook, Koryo Hand Acupuncture. In the third edition of his textbook, Koryo Hand

Therapy, the Correspondence Theory section was expanded, but still makes up only 57 pages of the 684 page book.

The logical layout of the map of the body on the hands allows it to be easily learned by almost anyone, including those who have no knowledge of acupuncture and even children. But in its simplicity lies an elegant and powerful treatment system.

Pain in the body manifests in the hands as tender points in the areas that represent that body part. Problems in the body can also produce changes in skin color or texture in the hands. Chronic problems can result in tense areas under the skin or small protrusions that can be seen or felt. Stimulation of these areas of the hands results in rapidly improved pain in the body. According to Dr. Yoo, it works the other way as well, with injuries to the hands causing problems in the corresponding areas of the body. I have no personal experience with this reverse effect, but I have become more protective of my hands around sharp objects. Perhaps it is because we have two hands that are unlikely to get injured in the same corresponding locations that we do not notice body problems after a hand injury.

Is Korean Hand Therapy Acupressure?

I am often asked this question when I tell people that Korean Hand Therapy is an acupuncture microsystem but the use of needles is not required. Many people incorrectly assume I am talking about body acupressure. They point to Large Intestine 4, an important acupuncture point between the thumb and index finger used to treat pain in the head and neck. I explain that Korean Hand Therapy is different, with a map of the entire body on both hands in addition to the acupuncture meridians and points, including a point analagous to Large Intestine 4.

Acupressure applies the same treatment protocols and points as acupuncture. Korean Hand Therapy has a unique system of treatment principles and theories, in addition to using acupuncture treatments on the hands. Both use blunt pressure as stimulation, but that is where the similarities end.

Is Korean Hand Therapy Reflexology?

There are commonalities between Correspondence Korean Hand Therapy and hand reflexology, as both involve treating specific areas of the hands with blunt pressure. However, Korean Hand Therapy is a complete acupuncture microsystem with advanced treatment protocols and the use of other techniques to stimulate the points, including press pellets, acupuncture needles, electrical stimulation, and moxa.

To me, reflexology seems incredibly complicated. Reflexology maps look like someone exploded a bomb in a human body and the parts scattered all over the hand or foot, with some of them duplicated in multiple areas. I often joke that reflexology clinics always have posters of reflexology maps on the walls because practitioners are unable to remember where the parts of the body are located and need to check the charts while they treat clients. In comparison, the Korean Hand Therapy map of the body on the hands is logical and easy to memorize.

How Common Is Korean Hand Therapy in the United States?

I truly believe Korean Hand Therapy is the best kept secret in pain management. Although it is well known in Korea and Japan, most acupuncturists and physicians in the United States know little to nothing about it. Unlike the ear and scalp acupuncture microsystems, Korean Hand Therapy is not part of the standard curriculum in most American acupuncture schools. Despite two chapters about Korean Hand Therapy in the sixth edition of the American Academy of Pain's textbook, Pain Management: A Practical Guide For Clinicians, most pain management experts in the United States have never heard of it.

Dan Lobash, PhD, LAc, an acupuncturist from California, who wrote one of the two chapters in the above mentioned textbook, learned Korean Hand Therapy when Dr. Yoo first came to California in 1988 to teach seminars. Since then, Dr. Lobash and his wife Geri, a nurse and acupuncturist, have traveled extensively across the United States teaching Korean Hand Therapy to acupuncturists and other healthcare professionals. If it was not for Dr. Lobash, Korean Hand Therapy would be almost unknown in the United States.

How Korean Hand Therapy Works

The Simple Answer: We Don't Know

If you are not a self-proclaimed science nerd or the kind of person who absolutely must know how things work before you will even consider trying them, PLEASE SKIP THIS CHAPTER. Yes, you read that correctly. Reading this chapter will not improve your ability to learn how to treat your own pain. It might also be counter-productive for you to get caught up in deep thoughts about how Korean Hand Therapy works before learning the system. The good news is you can always come back to this chapter and read it later if you choose.

I have taught Correspondence Korean Hand Therapy workshops to audiences of medical students, doctors, nurses, chiropractors and massage therapists. Many of the workshops have been accredited for continuing education hours for healthcare professionals, which require that they contain references to published research supporting the information that is presented. In general, healthcare professionals like knowing about the mechanism of action of a particular treatment, regardless of whether it is a pharmaceutical product, vitamin, herbal medicine, or surgical procedure before they can open their mind to the possibility that it might actually work. Over the years, I have been asked many times by doctors and nurses to explain to them how their pain has decreased after I poked on their hand. They have a hard time believing the results they have personally experienced. They find it hard to accept that the simple act of poking on tender points on their hand could have any effect on their body.

No one knows exactly how Korean Hand Therapy, or even acupuncture, works. I can provide some information about theories that may help explain the reductions in pain that occur, but I cannot prove that they are true. And, to be completely honest, how Korean Hand Therapy works is not important. After my personal experiences seeing dramatic and almost instantaneous improvements in pain and range of motion in so many people, I do not need any additional proof that it works. I know it works. It absolutely works. And it would not work any better or faster if I knew the exact mechanism by which it works. In many ways, this is similar to my relationship with my car. I know how to operate it but I do not have to be a car mechanic or have an understanding of what is happening under the hood in order to drive it.

The Homunculus

In medical school, everyone learns about the homunculus, which means "little man." Or, more correctly, the two homunculi (plural for homunculus) which are the representations of the parts of the brain dedicated to movement (motor function) and sensitivity to touch (sensory function).

Dr. Wilder Penfield was a neurosurgeon who used electrical current to stimulate specific areas of the brain and carefully recorded the effects noted in patients. This lead to a map of two slices of the cortex of the brain known as the motor cortex and sensory cortex. There are varying amounts of brain area dedicated to different parts of the body. Dr. Penfield also created a cartoon-like representations to illustrate the proportional amount of these sections of brain dedicated to different body parts. These are known as the motor homunculus and sensory homunculus.

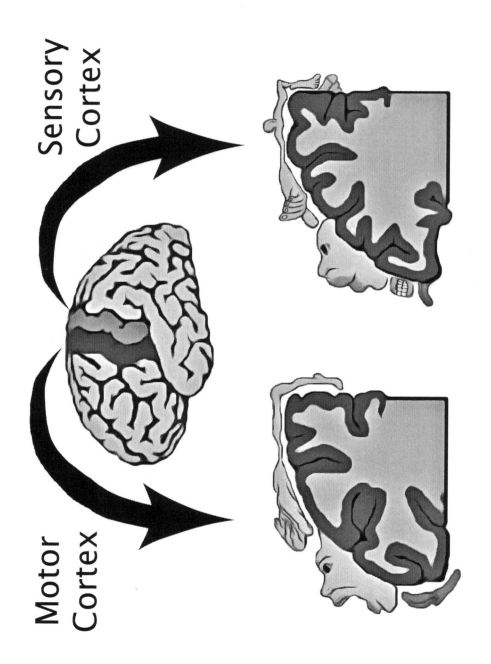

Original Homunculus Models

When I first saw the pictures of Dr. Penfield's motor homunculus and sensory homunculus in medical school, I was simultaneously drawn to and repulsed by the grotesque representation of the faces. To be honest, the faces were all I remembered because the drawings were so strange. The motor cortex was depicted as having a big open mouth with a protruding tongue due to the large area of the brain responsible for the intricate movements of our that allows us to talk and eat. The sensory cortex has large lips, eyes and genitals, corresponding to how these areas of the body are more sensitive to touch than others.

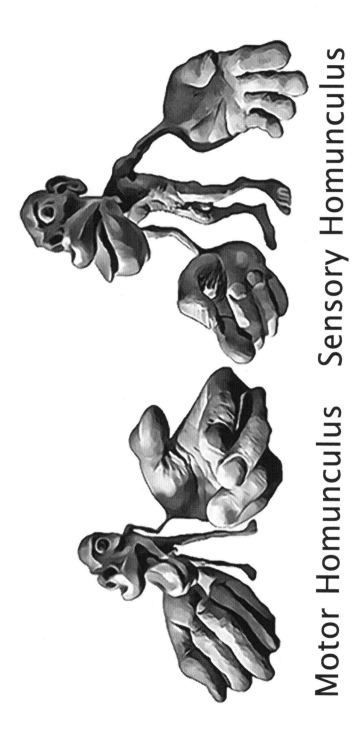

Sensory Homunculus

Motor Homunculus

Three Dimensional Homunculus Models

I did not recognize, until many years later while learning Korean Hand Therapy, that the hands of both the motor homunculus and sensory homunculus are huge. It was hard to believe that I did not notice them when I first saw these drawings because they are so disproportionately large and distorted. Actually, I did not notice the hands at all, until I saw the motor homunculus and sensory homunculus presented in three-dimensional models instead of the drawings that date back to Dr. Penfield. The three-dimensional models show how a person would look if their body developed based on the proportions of brain dedicated to each of those areas in the motor cortex and sensory cortex.

These new representations do not show the location on the brain for each area of the body, as the older diagrams do. However, when looking at the three-dimensional models, you cannot miss that the hands have more brain area dedicated to them than most other body parts. The hands on the sensory homunculus are large because we need to have sensitive hands to feel light touch or know if we are touching something too hot. The hands on the motor homunculus are even larger and allow us to do fine movements with our fingers in order to write, carefully pick up things, and perform detailed tasks.

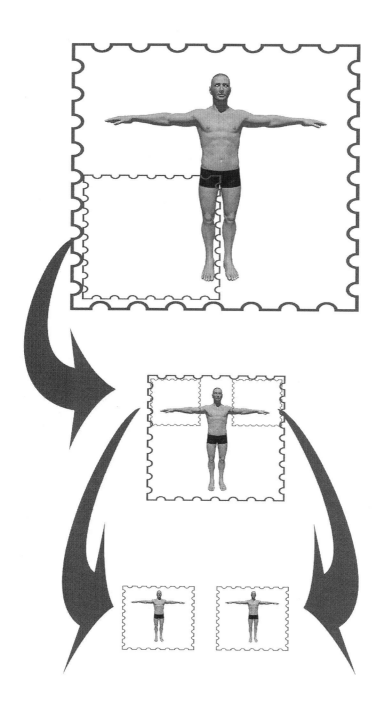

The Hand is a Hologram of the Body

This concept is a little more abstract. Because the entire body is represented on each hand, the hand is a hologram of the body. To better understand this idea, it is helpful to review how holograms work and their unique properties.

A normal photographic image of a person contains the information of the different parts of the body in different parts of the image. So if you cut a section off the picture of a person, the small piece only has the information from that part of the image. If you use a light to project the image, you will only see the part of the image you cut off.

Holograms are different. Every part of the picture is contained in every part of the image. So if you cut a section off a holographic image and project a laser through it, you will see the entire image. Even the smallest piece of the hologram contains the complete image. This may sound impossible, but it is a simplified description of how holograms work.

It may seem strange but there are other aspects of medicine that are similar to holograms, including our DNA. Every cell in our bodies contains the entire DNA sequence for our complete body, not just the organ that cell came from. So, each skin cell contains the complete 46 chromosomes necessary to recreate your entire body, not just the genetic code for your skin.

"Pain Is Brain"

Once you understand that the hands are represented on large areas of the brain, it becomes clear that Korean Hand Therapy works by affecting the brain through the hands. This is important because our sense of pain comes primarily from our brains.

Even with similar physical injuries, different people perceive pain differently. If I step on the toes of several people with the same force, some of them might scream, some might complain a little, and others might barely even notice it. The injury itself does not determine how much pain we feel and how it impacts our life. The experience of pain comes from the way the pain signal is interpreted by the brain. It involves not only the type and severity of the injury. but also any emotional association it may have based on our past experiences with pain. This also explains how people with missing limbs still feel pain in parts of their bodies that are no longer there.

When a point on the hand is stimulated with Korean Hand Therapy, a signal travels to the brain along the nerves between them. The slight discomfort of poking on the points helps propel this signal along these pathways designed to quickly transmit pain, which perhaps contributes to the rapid effects. Because a large part of the brain is affected by stimulating a tiny area on the hands, a significant reduction in pain results from such a small action. This may also explain how poking on just a few hand points can reduce pain in large areas of the body.

Korean Hand Therapy Research

Unfortunately, most of the research on Korean Hand Therapy is not published in English language medical journals because most of the studies are done in Korea or Japan. Some of the research abstracts (short summaries that are usually only a paragraph long) are available in English but the details of the study design, methods and findings are published in another language. Most of the studies do not evaluate the use of Correspondence Korean Hand Therapy, but instead use protocols based on advanced forms of Korean Hand Therapy. At the biannual Korean Hand Therapy conference in South Korea, research presentations are done in Korean or Japanese with simultaneous translation in those languages only.

During my workshops that are accredited for continuing education hours, I discuss published research that supports the use of Korean Hand Therapy and provide the references in case attendees wish to review the scientific information in greater detail. Because I want this book to accurately reflect what I teach in the workshops, I am including the the same discussion of some of the research here. There is a more extensive list of some of the published research studies at the end of this book.

Korean Hand Acupressure Reduces Postoperative Vomiting in Children After Strabismus Surgery

Double-blind, randomized trial. 50 children aged 3–12 yo. Excluded gastric or intestinal diseases, emesis and vomiting in week before surgery	n	Incidence of Vomiting in 24 hrs
Treatment applied 30 min prior to anesthesia		
Treatment Group	25	20% 5 patients (P=0.001)
Placebo Group: Tape Only - No Disc	25	68 % 17 patients
Two children in the treatment group and 10 children in the placebo group required antiemetic rescue therapy		

Schlager A., et al. *Br J Anaesth.* 2000 Aug;85(2):267-270.

Korean hand acupressure reduces postoperative vomiting in children after strabismus surgery. Schlager A, Boehler M, Pühringer F. Br J Anaesth. 2000 Aug;85(2):267-270.

This study is particularly interesting, as it was a double-blind, randomized controlled trial published in the British Journal of Anaesthesia. It evaluated a group of children undergoing eye surgery. Nausea and vomiting is common with strabismus surgery and the researchers decided to study a single intervention in order to reduce the incidence of vomiting in the 24 hours following surgery.

In 25 children, a single press pellet with tape was applied to a point on the palm side of both ring fingers 30 minutes prior to surgery. The point used is called K9 in Korean Hand Therapy. This point corresponds to the body acupuncture point Pericardium 6 or Nei Guan, which is commonly used for treating nausea and vomiting. The study's control group of 25 children had a similar appearing tape applied to the same points without press pellets. Neither the investigators nor the patients knew which treatment they were given. Children with pre-existing gastrointestinal problems or vomiting in the week prior to surgery were excluded from the study.

The study investigators reported that the incidence of vomiting in the 24 hours after surgery was statistically less in the group receiving the Korean Hand Therapy treatment versus the control group. They also noted that fewer patients in the Korean Hand Therapy group required medication to treat nausea and vomiting.

After the study was published, the results were felt to be too good to be true. Many people could not believe that two pellets on the fingers could reduce vomiting. Some of the critics said that the outcome was a fluke and probably did not reflect a true effect of such a simple intervention. Others speculated that the results in a pediatric population could not be generalized to adults because kids were physiologically different. Some also expressed concerns that nausea after eye surgery might be different than other types of nausea and the results could not be extrapolated to other surgeries.

The location of the Korean Hand Therapy point K9 and the corresponding Pericardium 6 acupuncture point on the body are shown on the next page. Wrist bands that apply pressure to the Pericardium 6 point are sold to treat nausea due to motion sickness or pregnancy. Applying press pellets to K9 on the hand produces the same effect.

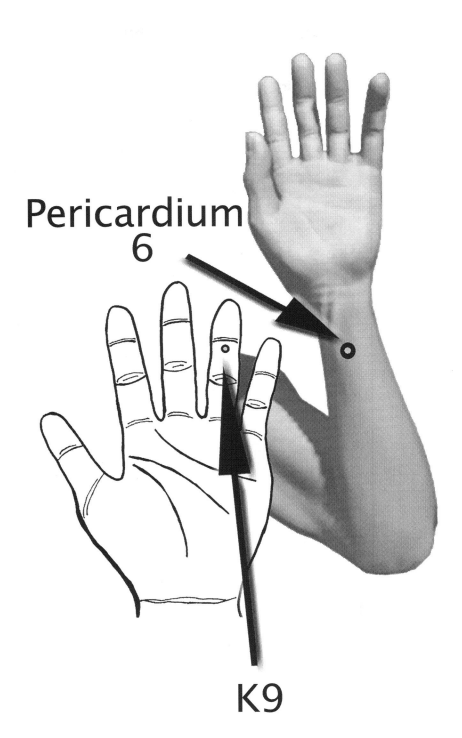

Pericardium
6

K9

Korean Hand Acupressure Reduces Postoperative Nausea And Vomiting After GYN Laparoscopic Surgery

Treatment applied 30 min prior to anesthesia	N	Incidence of Nausea in 24 hrs	Incidence of Vomiting in 24 hrs
Treatment Group	40	40% 16 patients ($P=0.007$)	22.5% 9 patients ($P=0.006$)
Placebo Group: Tape Only - No Disc	40	70% 28 patients	50% 20 patients

Boehler M, et al. *Anesth Analg.* 2002 Apr;94(4):872-875.

Korean hand acupressure reduces postoperative nausea and vomiting after gynecological laparoscopic surgery. Boehler M, Mitterschiffthaler G, Schlager A. Anesth Analg. 2002 Apr;94(4):872-875.

The investigators from the previously discussed study did a similar second study in women undergoing laparoscopic gynecological surgery. The findings were published in another Western medical journal of anesthesia.

The second study was also different in that the investigators wanted to know if there was also difference in the incidence of nausea reported by the patients during the first 24 hours after surgery. In this study, 40 women had a press pellet with tape applied to the Korean Hand Therapy point K9 on both hands. The 40 women in the control group had only the tape applied to the same area of both hands. Again, neither the patients nor the investigators knew which patients had press pellets before the study ended.

As in the first study, there was a statistically significant decrease in the incidence of vomiting in the 24 hours following surgery in the Korean Hand Therapy group versus the control group. There was also a statistically significant decrease in the incidence of nausea reported by patients in the Korean Hand Therapy group during that time.

Prevention of Postoperative Sore Throat Using Capsicum Plaster

Double-blind, randomized trial. Excluded known difficult airways or multiple intubations attempts required.

Pain scale used: 0 none/1 minimal/2 mild/3 moderate/ 4 severe

Total Abdominal Hysterectomy Patients receiving same pre/post op anesthesia	n	Pain in Recovery	Pain 24 hrs Later
Treatment Group – Capsicum on A20, Tape on Thighs	50	3	0*#
Sham Group: Tape on A20, Capsicum on Thighs	50	3	2*
Placebo Group: Tape on A20 & Thighs	50	3	2*

$*p = 0.00068$ vs RR, $\#p = 0.00027$ vs Sham and Placebo

Park HS, et al. Anaesthesia. 2004; 59(7):647–651.

Prevention of postoperative sore throat using capsicum plaster applied at the Korean hand acupuncture point. Park HS, Kim KS, Min HK, Kim DW. Anaesthesia. 2004; 59(7):647–651.

Sore throat is a common side effect after being intubated for general anesthesia. This study looked at 150 women undergoing the same total abdominal hysterectomy procedure. Patients were excluded from the study if they were known to have difficulty being intubated or if multiple attempts were required to intubated them.

Instead of press pellets, this study used a small plaster containing capsicum, the component of chili peppers that causes local irritation of the skin. The research focused on the Korean Hand Therapy point A20, which is the Suprasternal Notch in Correspondence Korean Hand Therapy and is where the endotracheal tube passes through the larynx when patients are intubated.

The research design of this study was more complicated, with three treatment arms and 50 patients in each group. The Treatment group had the capsicum plaster placed on A20 of both hands and a plain piece of tape applied to both thighs. The second group was called the Sham treatment group because they had a treatment that should not work - capsicum plasters applied to both thighs and a plain piece of tape on both A20 points. A third group was a true Placebo group, with plain tape applied to both A20 points and plain tape on both thighs. During the study, the patients did not know what treatment they had been given and the investigators did not know which treatment group the patients were in.

Sore throat pain was reported by the patients using a simple pain scale ranging from 0 to 4. All three groups reported the same average throat pain score of 3, or moderate pain, in the recovery room after surgery.

At 24 hours after surgery, the treatment group with the capsicum plaster at the A20 point had average throat pain scores of 0 while the other two groups had average throat pain scores of 2, or mild pain. For the treatment group, this represented both a statistically significant change from their own throat pain scores in recovery and in comparison to both the sham treatment and placebo groups at 24 hours.

There was no difference in the amounts of pain medication and no difference in rates of nausea, vomiting or coughing between the three groups in the first 24 hours. The only side effect noted was mild burning and redness in 2 patients with capsicum plasters on their fingers and 4 patients with capsicum plasters on their thighs which resolved within a day after removal.

The location of the A20 point, corresponding to the Supreasternal Notch on the body, is shown on the next page.

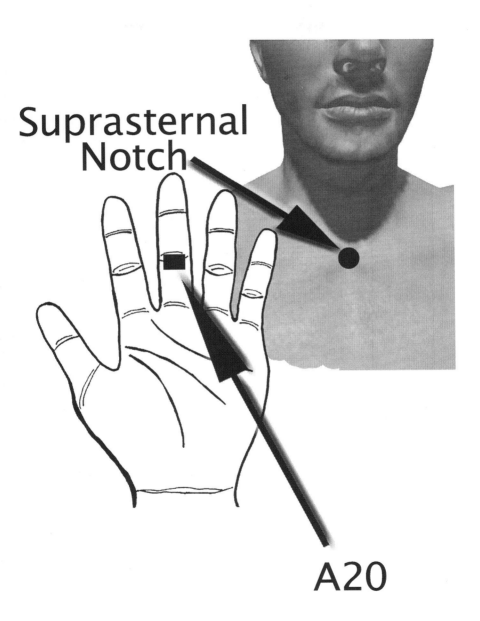

Suprasternal Notch

A20

Hand acupuncture experience in pediatric patients. Jodorkovsky R. Medical Acupuncture. 1999;11(1):25-28.

Dr. Roberto Jodorkovsky published his experience with using Korean Hand Therapy in his pediatric practice in Maryland. He reported that he had used this approach with over 100 patients with pain or chronic conditions. All of the patients were treated using Correspondence Therapy and the more complicated cases were treated with advanced Korean Hand Therapy techniques in addition. The most common problems that he treated with Korean Hand Therapy were sore throat, pain in knees, wrists, hands, ankles or feet, and asthma. He reported that 96% of the patients responded to treatment with Korean Hand Therapy. 70% had improved symptoms within 3 days and all patients tolerated the treatments well.

The Map of the Body on Your Hands

Orientation to the Map

Every map has a key indicating which direction on the map is north, so you can get your bearings. When I teach Correspondence Korean Hand Therapy, the hands are always held upright, with the fingers straight and pointing upwards. The palm side of the hands are always facing outward when you are figuring out what hand and fingers to use. Just as you would not read a map upside down, you should not look at your hands in any other position if you want to maintain your orientation. Always looking at your hands in this upright position makes it easy to quickly identify key landmarks on the hand and to easily locate the search zones.

Do not get overwhelmed with the information presented in this chapter. Some of it may not make sense until you go through the rest of the book and learn the map of the body on the hands. Come back to this chapter anytime you would like to review it.

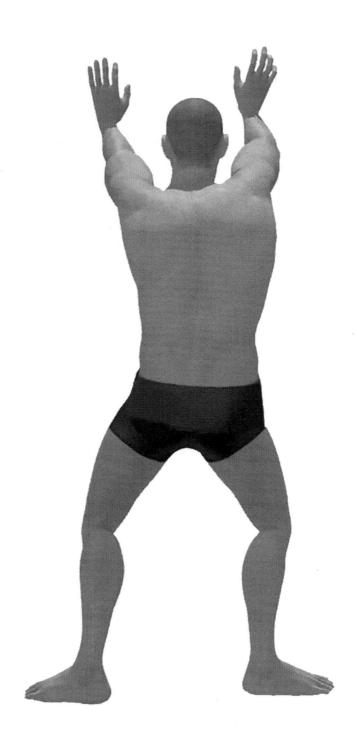

Assume the Position -
Hands and Feet Upward

To best represent the location of the map of the body on the hands held upright, you would ideally be seated. Both arms would be raised up next to your head and both legs would be elegantly stretched up alongside the arms, in a perfect yoga pose. A body in this position would best mimic a hand with the fingers all pointed upward. But since most of us cannot manage this tricky pose, standing with your arms raised while imagining your legs are upright is the next best option. Remember to keep your knees and toes pointed outward when standing, to remind you that the inner thighs and inner lower legs are represented on the palm side of the hands.

Arms and Legs
Are Raised and Rotated Outward

When trying to determine if problem is located on the front or back of the body, it is helpful to remember that the map of the body on the hand has the arms and legs raised. This reminds us that the inner aspects of the arms and legs are on the front of the body. When you raise your arms above your head, it is easy to see that the underside of your arms and the palms of your hands are facing forward, and therefore are represented on the palm side of the hand. The backs of your hands and the backs of your arms are represented on the back side of the hand.

The legs are a bit trickier because most of us cannot raise our feet over our heads. If you are seated or standing, the feet should be turned out with the knees and toes pointing outward. In this position, the inner thighs and calves are facing forward to remind us that they are on the front of the body, and therefore represented on the palm side of the hand. Imagine a frog lying on his back, making it easy to see what part of the legs are on the front side of his body. The outer thighs and calves are rotated backward because they are on the back of the body, and therefore are represented on the back side of the hand. The soles of the feet would be facing forward if your legs were raised above your head and therefore are represented on the palm side of the hand. The back side of the foot is represented on the back side of the hand.

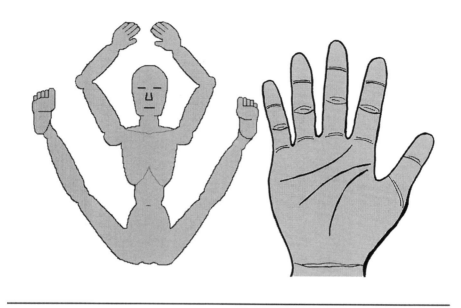

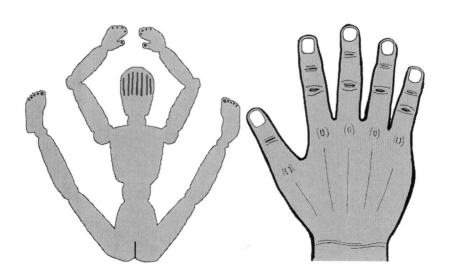

Front and Back of the Hands
Are Front and Back of the Body

Problems that are located on the front of the body are represented on the palm side of the hand, where the fingerprints and palms are. Problems that are located on the back of the body are represented on the back of the hand, where the nails and knuckles are. Problems located between the front and back of the body, are located on the sides of the fingers or hand.

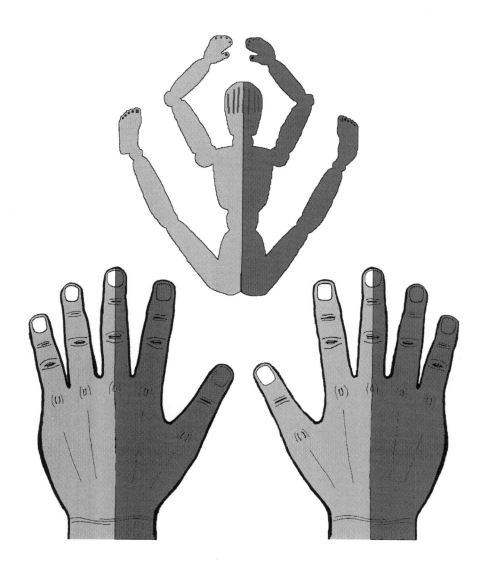

Three of You In A Row

Stand up with both your hands upright and palms facing forward. In this position, it is as if there are three versions of you in a row - you in the center, and your two hand "clones" on either side. The body is represented in its entirety on both hands.

Imagine a line down the center of the middle finger of each hand. The right side of your body is represented on the right side of the right hand and on the right side of the left hand. Similarly, the left side of your body is represented on the left side of the left hand and the left side of the right hand. This goes for the front of the body as well as the back of the body.

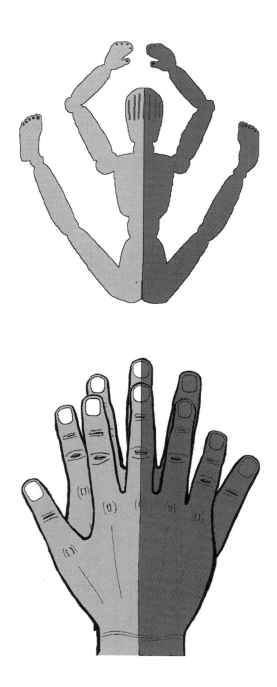

One Hand On Top of the Other

Another way to remember how both hands represent the left and right sides of the body is to place one hand on top of the other, with the backs of the hands facing you. It does not matter if you do it with the right hand or the left hand on top. With your hands lined up this way, imagine that there is a line drawn down the middle of the middle finger. On both hands, everything on the right side of the line represents the right side of your body and everything on the left side of the line represents the left side of your body.

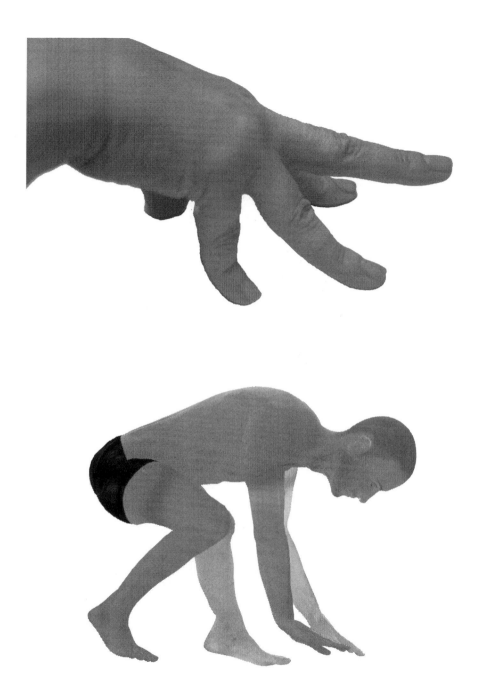

Crawling Animal/Crouching Man

When you first learn Correspondence Korean Hand Therapy, it is easy to get confused about which fingers represent the arms and which fingers represent the legs. By making a figure with your hand on a flat surface that looks like a little four-legged animal or crouching man, it all becomes clear. The middle finger is the head and neck and is the only finger that does not touch the surface. With your hand in this position, it is easy to recognize that the fingers on either side of the middle finger (the index and ring fingers) are the arms and the fingers furthest away from the middle finger (the thumb and pinky fingers) are the legs. You can make a crouching man or crawling animal anytime you get a little mixed up about what finger should be used.

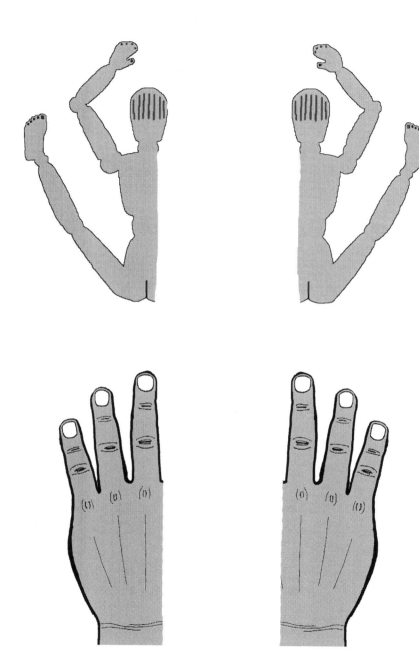

Focus on the 3 Outer Fingers

To further simplify things, focus on the three outer fingers of both hands - the middle, ring and pinky fingers. Right sided body problems should be treated with the right hand and left sided body problems should be treated with the left hand. Body problems in the center of the body (head, neck, mid-abdomen, and mid-back) can be treated using either hand but in the beginning, stick with the same-sided hand as the problem in your body. Once you get a bit more experienced with this system, you can use your non-dominant hand to treat pain that is in the center of the body because it is easier to apply pressure to locate and treat points using your dominant hand.

The thumb and index finger only need to be used in rare circumstances when you cannot use the hand that is on the same side of the body problem. For example, if someone has pain on the right side of their body but they do not have a right hand, they need to use the left hand to treat the pain. Or if a right hand has been seriously injured with extensive scar tissue or nerve damage, it is best to use the left hand to treat problems on the right side of the body. Another example of when not to use the hand on the same side of the body is in people who have lymphedema of the upper extremity following mastectomy (removal of the breast, usually for cancer), with chronic swelling due to reduced lymph drainage. They are advised not to allow blood testing or blood pressure readings on that limb because of the increased risk of infection. In such cases, it would be best to use the thumb, index and middle fingers of the hand on the opposite side of the body problem.

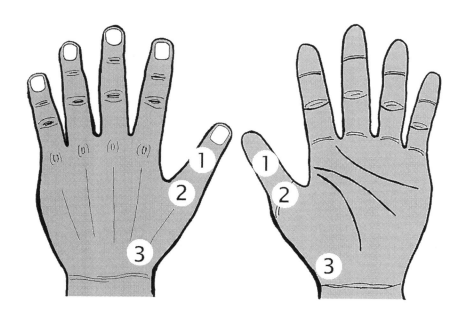

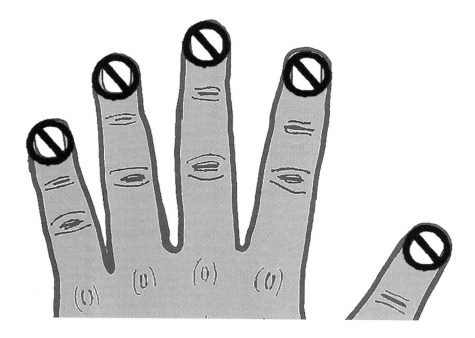

The Thumb Is Weird

The middle, ring, and pinky fingers are used most of the time because treating pain using the hand on the same side as the body pain works better. But another reason to avoid the thumb and index fingers is the strange shape of the thumb.

The joints of the thumb are not where most people would think they are. Take a look at your thumb with the hand in an upright position. The first joint is easy to locate. The second joint is where the thumb attaches to the palm. And the third joint? It is buried down in the base of the palm. If you follow the index finger all the way down to the wrist, you will find the third joint of the thumb deep within the muscles at the bottom of the hand.

Avoid the Nails

The nails are areas of the hand that cannot be used in Korean Hand Therapy. Pressing on them does not relieve pain and can damage the nails. You cannot directly access the back of the head (on the middle finger), backs of the hands (on the ring and index fingers) or backs of the feet (on the thumb and pinky fingers). If you have pain in these areas of your body, you must search for points around the margins of the nails, not directly on them. Another option is to check the palm side of the fingertips to see if you can find tender points to use instead.

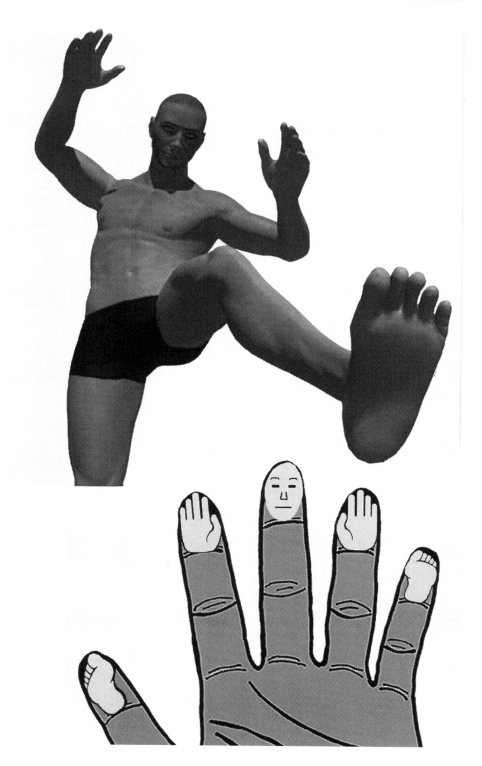

Thumbs and Big Toes
Point Toward the Head

The palms of both hands are represented on the palm side of your hand, on the tips of the ring and index fingers. The soles of both feet are represented on the palm side of your hand, on the tips of the pinky finger and thumb. It is important to remember the orientation of the hands and feet on the fingertips to be able to accurately locate corresponding points in cases of hand or foot pain.

If you raise both your arms up alongside your head with the palms facing forward, both of your thumbs will be close to your head. This is the same way the hands are projected onto the ring and index fingers. The thumbs are located on the inner sides of the ring and index fingertips, close to the middle finger. The pinky fingers are located on the outer edge of the ring fingertip (next to the pinky finger on your hand) and the outer edge of the index fingertip (next to the thumb on your hand).

If you were able to also raise both your legs up alongside your head with the soles of the feet facing forward, both of your big toes would be close to your arms, This is the same way the feet are projected onto the pinky finger and thumb. The big toes are located on the inner side of the pinky fingertip (next to the ring fingertip) and the inner side of the thumb (next to the index fingertip). The pinky toes are located on the outer edge of the pinky fingertip and on the outer edge of the tip of the thumb.

Looking at Your Hand Is Not
the Same as Looking in the Mirror

When your hand is held in front of your face with the palm facing you, it is easy to get confused about what part of the hand represents the left and right sides of the body. We are used to looking at ourselves in a mirror, so it is easy to incorrectly assume that we are looking at ourselves when we ponder our palms. Therefore, it is always best to first start with your hands raised on either side of your body so that the left and right distinction is clear. Once you determine which hand to use and which part of the hand needs to be searched, bring the hand front of you to begin searching for specific points.

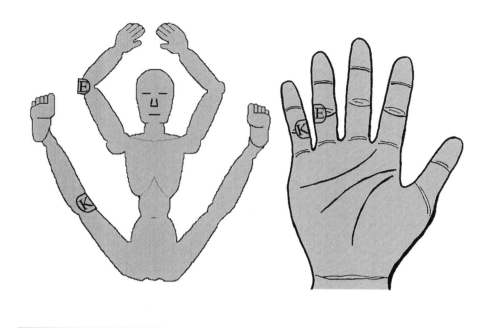

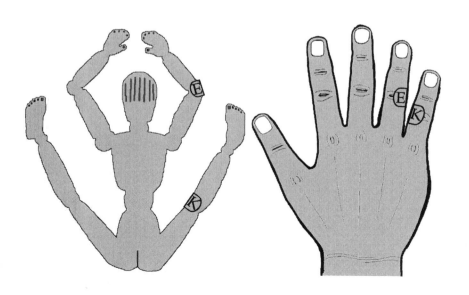

Elbows and Knees Are on the Sides of Fingers

Another important thing to note is where the bony parts of the elbows and the kneecaps are represented on the hands. Raising your arms above your head again helps demonstrate that our elbows jut outward, away from the head. They are represented on the outer edges of the index and ring fingers in the same way. Half of the bony part of the elbow is on the palm side of the finger and half of the bony part of the elbow is on the back side of the finger.

The kneecaps need to be considered as if the legs were also raised up toward the head. The legs naturally rotate when raised up and the knees point toward the head. Therefore, they are represented on the inner aspects of the pinky finger and thumb. Half of the kneecap is on the palm side of the finger and half of the kneecap is on the back side of the finger.

When looking at the map of the body on the hands, notice that the bony part of the elbow on the outer margin of the ring finger bumps up against the kneecap on the inner margin of the pinky finger. This is true on both the palm and back sides of the hands.

Notes:_____

_____

_____

_____

_____

_____

_____

_____

_____

_____

_____

_____

_____

_____

_____

_____

_____

_____

_____

_____

_____

_____

_____

_____

_____

_____

_____

_____

_____

_____

_____

_____

_____

The Center of the Body

Knowing which parts of the hand correspond to key locations on the front and back of the body is the secret to learning how to manage your own pain with Korean Hand Therapy. This chapter is full of diagrams that will present this information in a step-by-step manner, so you learn it with ease. This chapter focuses on the center of the body - the head, neck, chest, back, and abdomen. The next three chapters will cover the details of the head, arms and legs.

Once you master the landmarks of the body on the hands, you will be able to locate the areas on your hands to treat your pain without needing to refer to a chart. Always start by looking at your hands in the upright position, with the palms facing outward. The landmarks are easy to memorize if you always start with this orientation.

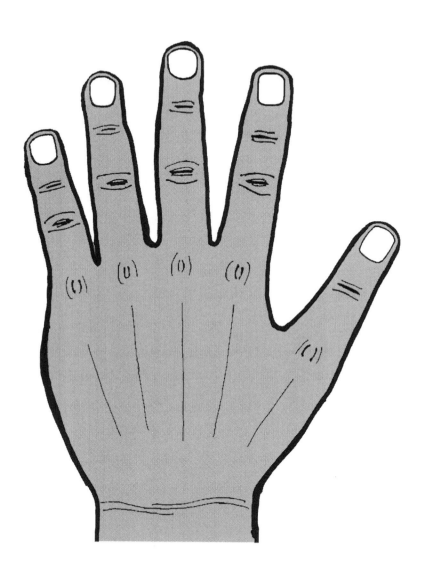

Starting with your hand in the upright position, inspect the back of your hand. Either hand will work, but we will use the left hand as the example in this book.

Look at the back of the middle, ring and pinky fingers. Notice how the creases at the first joints (closest to the nails) have fewer creases and a different pattern of creases than those at the second joints. The centers of the first joints - the spaces where two bones meet - are in the center of each group of creases. The centers of the second joints are in the center of each group of creases.

The third joints are more commonly known as knuckles and have a different appearance that the more distal joints. The centers of the third joints are at the highest peaks of each knuckle protrusion. Also note that there are no distinctive landmarks between the third joints and the wrist on the back of the hand.

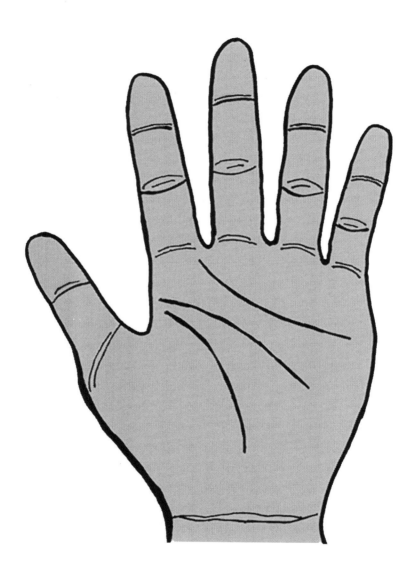

Now turn your hand over to look at the palm side. Again, start at the first joints that are closest to the fingertips. Notice how few creases there are at the first joints compared to the complicated tangle of creases at the second joints. The centers of the first joints are where several creases come together to create the fold where the fingertip bends. The centers of the second joints are at the lowest part of the group of creases and are best found by bending the fingers.

The third joints on the palm side of the hand are not where you might first think. They are NOT located at the creases where the fingers meet the palm, but rather in the top of the palm itself. Verify this yourself by putting the index finger of your other hand on a knuckle of any finger on the back of your hand and your thumb on the area below the same finger on the palm side. Flap your fingers back and forth to feel the third joint move from inside the palm. This will be important to remember as we go through the corresponding locations of the arms and legs on the hand. Just as on the back of the hand, notice that there are no distinctive landmarks between the third joints and the wrist on the palm side of the hand.

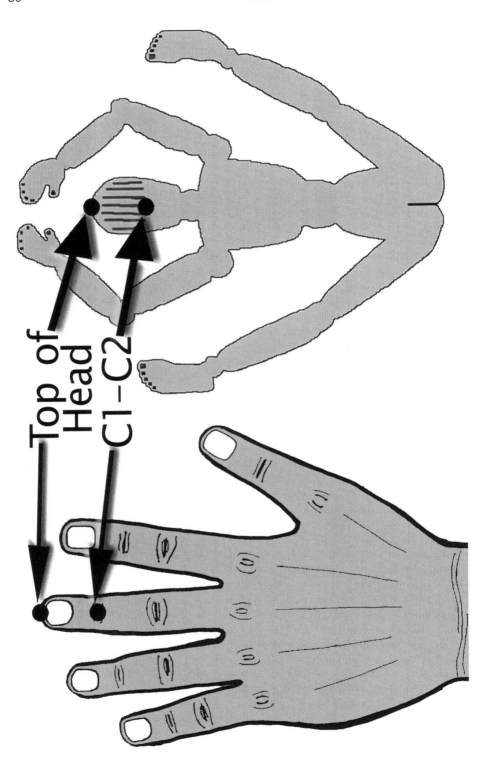

Top of
Head

C1 – C2

Back of the Body = Back of the Hand

The first joint on the middle finger represents the occiput or back of the head, where the skull curves inward and the spine enters the base of the skull. It is also the area between the Cervical 1 (C1) and Cervical 2 (C2) vertebrae of the upper neck. Some people have a prominent ridge on their skull in this area.

The top of the finger to the first joint on the middle finger represents the back of the head. Because much of this area is covered by the nail, it is difficult to locate tender points that correspond to the pain on the upper part of the back of the head. More details about the back of the middle fingertip are discussed in the the next chapter.

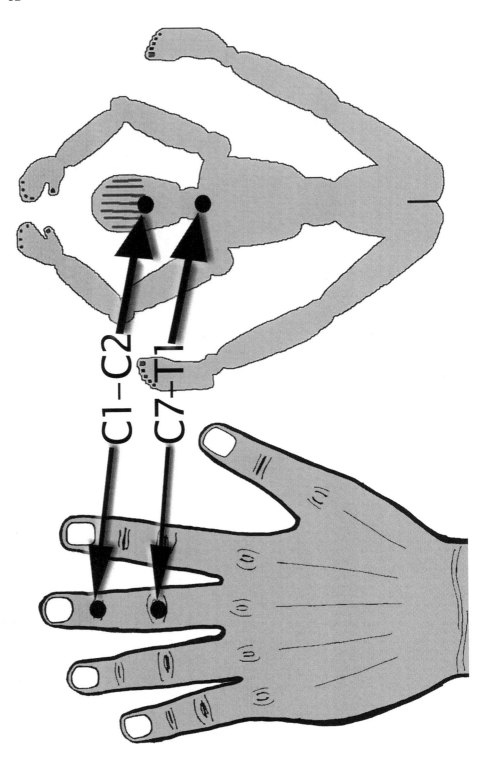

The second joint of the middle finger represents the area where the lower neck connects to the trunk of the body. This is the space between the Cervical 7 (C7) and Thoracic 1 (T1) vertebrae. The area between the first and second joints on the back side of the middle finger represents the back of the neck.

Most people have a prominent part of the spine at C7 when the neck is flexed forward that helps distinguish it from the other cervical vertebrae. You may feel movement in the C7 vertebrae when the neck is rotated from side to side. The T1 vertebrae below it does not move when the neck is rotated.

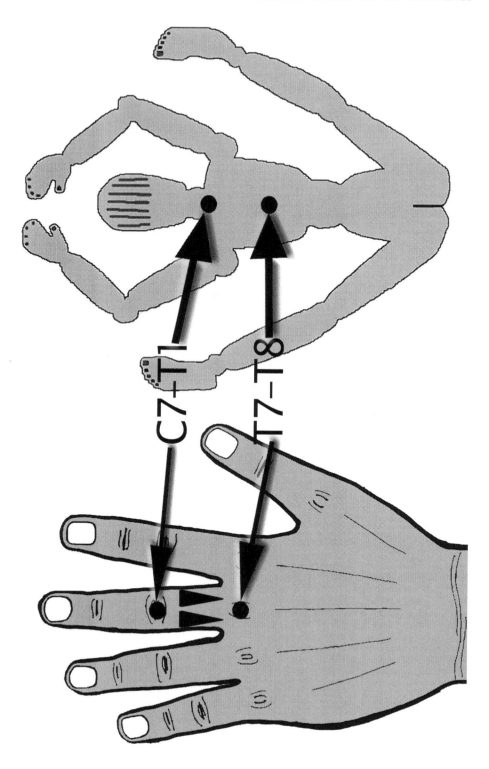

The third joint of the middle finger is on the knuckle. It corresponds to the space between the Thoracic 7 (T7) and Thoracic 8 (T8) vertebrae. This is the middle of the upper back and is approximately where a bra crosses the back in women.

The scapulas, or shoulder blades, are also in this area. The top of the scapulas are one quarter of the way down between C7-T1 and T7-T8 and continue as triangular shapes that taper off just above the T7-T8 area. Picturing the scapulas as two triangles in this area is helpful to remind you where to search for pain that is located above, between or on top of the shoulder blades.

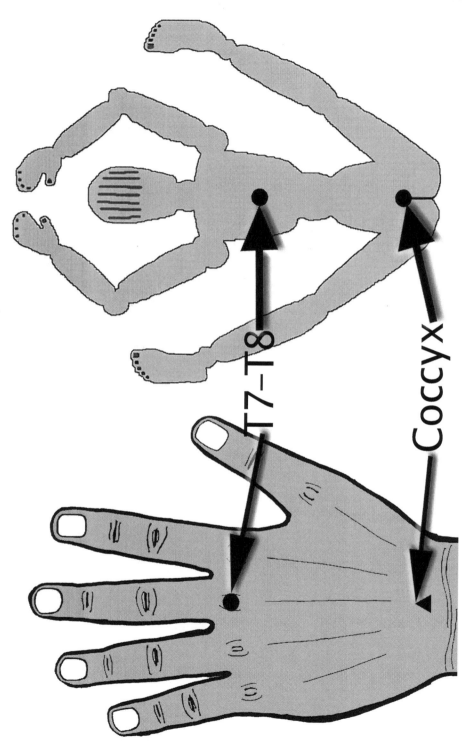

T7–T8

Coccyx

There are no clear landmarks on the back side of the hand so the next area to locate is further down by the wrist. Imagine a line drawn down the center of the middle finger. Before the line reaches the wrist, there is a deep depression that is triangle shaped. The top of that triangle represents the coccyx or tailbone. Many people who have previously injured their coccyx note that this point is tender on the hand.

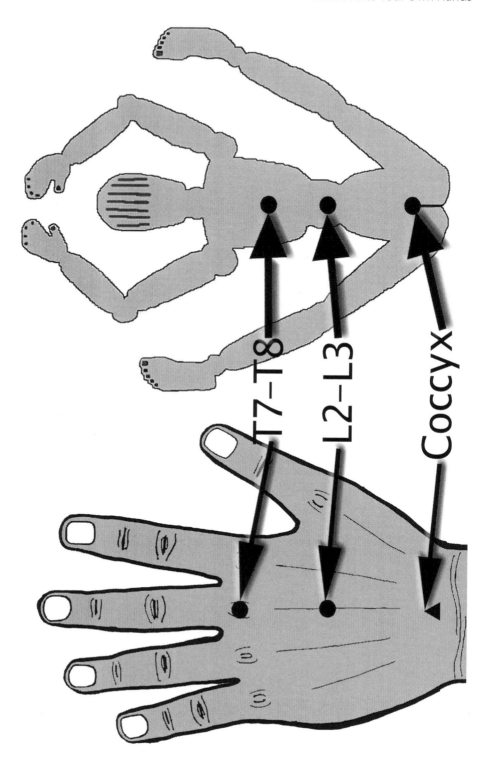

Halfway between the location of the T7-T8 vertebrae on the knuckle of the middle finger and the coccyx near the wrist is the area that represents the L2-L3 lumbar vertebrae. This is an important area to identify because many people have back pain at this low back area or below it.

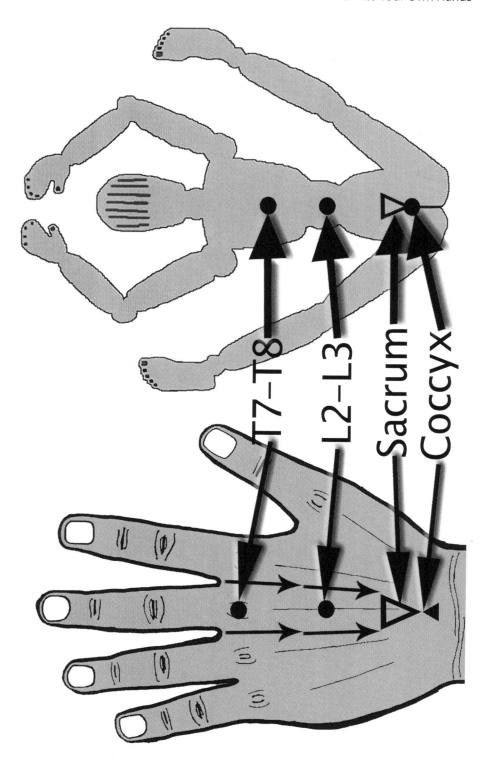

The sacrum can be identified by dragging the tip of your finger or a pen down both sides of the middle finger. As you approach the bottom of the backside of the hand, the bones in the hand flare out and you cannot go any further toward the wrist. These two points represent the left and right sides of the top of the sacrum. If you locate the coccyx and connect all three points, you will be able to outline the entire sacrum.

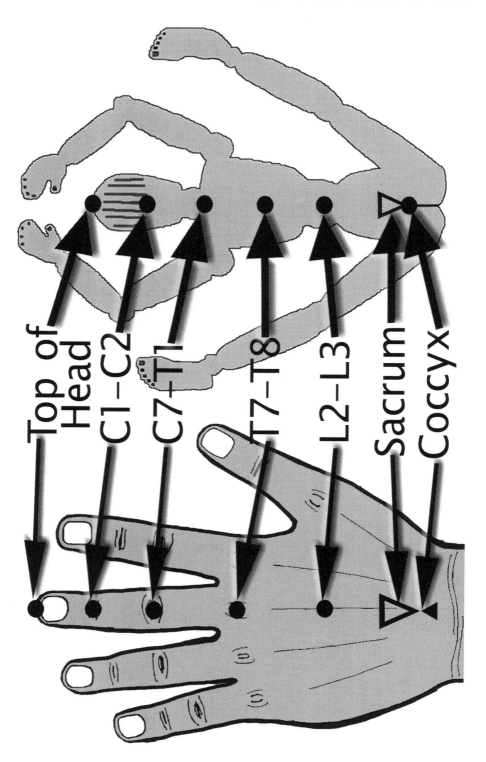

Top of Head

C1–C2

C7–T1

T7–T8

L2–L3

Sacrum

Coccyx

When you look at the map of the back of the center of the body, it is easy to see how logically everything is laid out on the hand. Once you become familiar with these landmarks on the back of the hand, you will be able to locate the areas that correspond to pain anywhere on the back of your head and neck and your entire back.

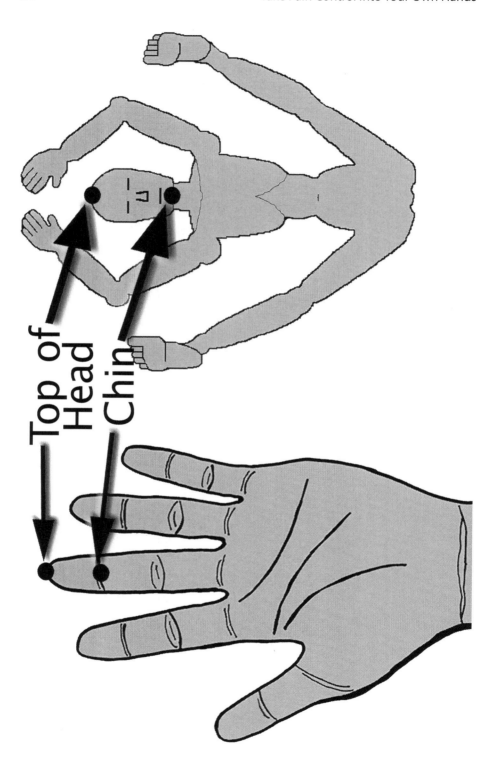

Top of
Head

Chin

Front of the Body = Palm of the Hand

The top of the head is represented on the tip of the middle finger, just a few millimeters in front of the nail. The group of creases on the first joint on the palm side of the middle finger represents the chin. It also represents the upper part of the front of the neck. In cases of sore throat, painful points can be identified just below the first crease on the palm side of the middle finger.

The palm side of the tip of the middle finger represents the face and the back of the tip of the middle finger represents the back of the head. Details about the representations of the face on the tip of the middle finger are in the next chapter.

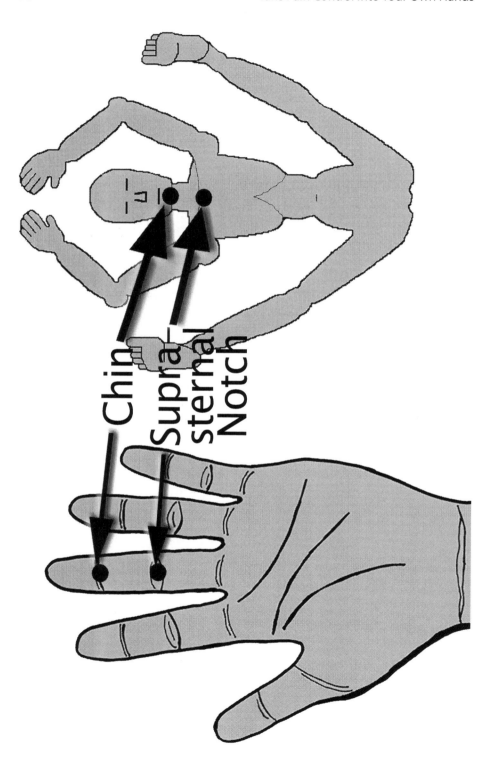

Chin

Supra-
sternal
Notch

The group of creases at the second joint on the palm side of the middle finger represents the Suprasternal Notch, which is the area where the clavicles (or collarbones) meet in the center of the lower neck. If you walk your fingers along the tops of your collarbones toward the center, you will find this indentation, where they come together in the midline of the neck.

The area between the first and second joints on the palm side of the middle finger represents the front of the neck. This mirrors the area between the first two joints on the back side of the middle finger that represents the back of the neck.

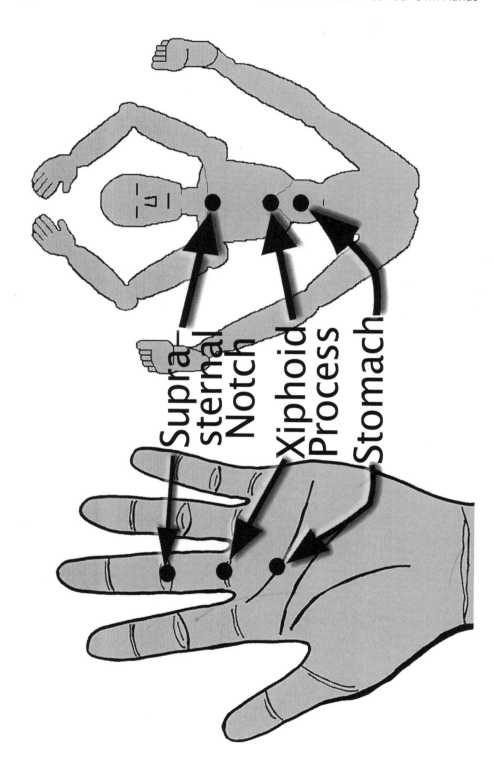

The next landmark on the middle finger can be confusing. In the chapters that follow this one, you will learn that the third joints on the palm side of the hands do not have a set of creases associated with them, as the first and second joints do. The third joints on the palm side of the hands are large and are located in the palm itself, not at the creases where the fingers meet the palm.

For the middle finger, we are making an exception and the third landmark we are looking for is where the middle finger meets the palm. The third group of creases on the palm side of the middle finger are at the top of the third joint in this spot. This represents the area in the middle of the chest known as the xiphoid process. If you walk your fingers along the lower rib margins towards the center of the front of the body, they meet in the center of the lower chest at this point. So the area between the second and third groups of creases on the palm side of the middle finger represents the chest and includes the heart, lungs and breasts.

The stomach is represented on the hand below this area, at the bottom of the third joint where there is a prominent crease running across the palm. It is not a landmark used to locate points that correspond to pain in the body, but it can be used to treat stomach discomfort, including indigestion if you have eaten too much.

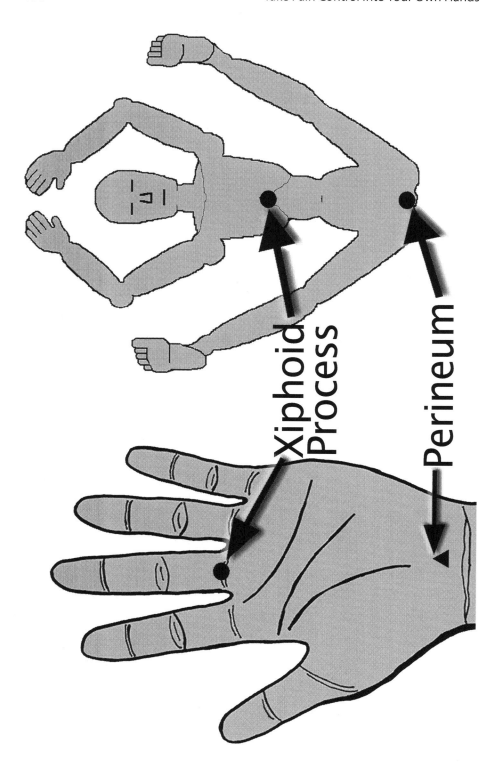

Xiphoid Process

Perineum

There are no clear landmarks in the palm of the hand, so we will skip down to an area just above the wrist. Imagine a line drawn down the middle of the middle finger. Before the line reaches the wrist creases, there is an area where the rounded muscles on either side of the lower palm come together. This area represents the Perineum, or the area between the sex organs and the rectum on the body. The way the muscles curve inward looks like the top of an upside down heart. The distance between the Perineum point and the wrist creases can vary from a few millimeters to half a centimeter above the wrist creases. There is a slight depression in the specific point that can be found with pressure from your finger or the tip of a pen.

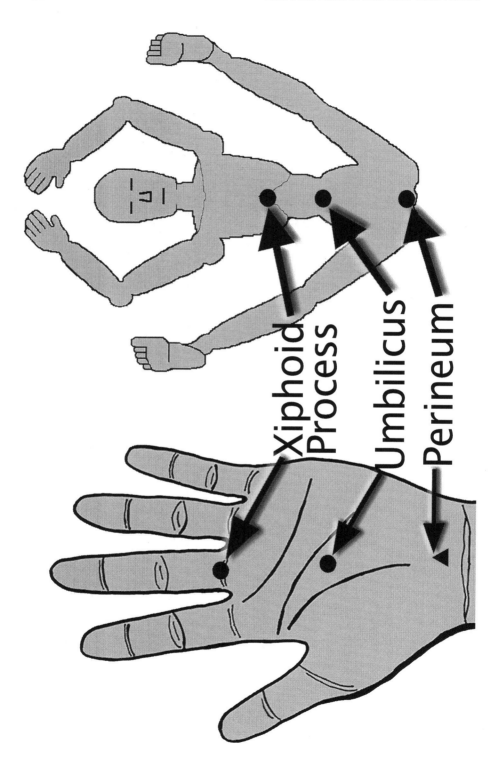

Halfway between the third creases on the palm side of the hand representing the Xiphoid Process and the area near the wrist that represents the Perineum is a point in the middle of the palm that represents the Umbilicus or Belly-button. This point itself is not used to treat pain, but it is an important landmark for locating points that correspond to pain in the upper and lower abdomen. The large intestine is located above and on both sides of the umbilicus. The ovaries, uterus and bladder are below the umbilicus.

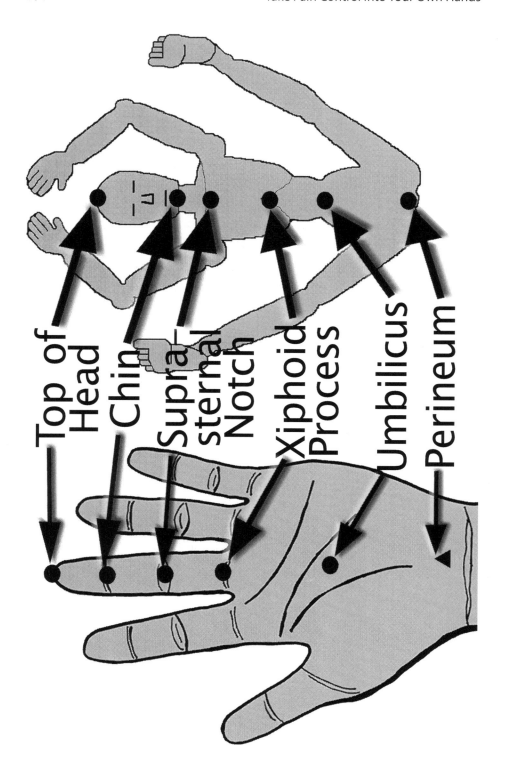

When you look at the map of the front of the center of the body, it is easy to see how logically everything is laid out on the palm side of the hand. Once you become familiar with these landmarks on the palm side of the hand, you will be able to locate the areas that correspond to pain in your face, front of the neck, chest, abdomen and pelvis.

Notes:_____

The Head

As described in the previous chapter, the palm side of the fingertip of the middle finger represents the head on your body. Because pain and problems on the head are common, it is important to have a good understanding of how to locate specific parts of the head on the fingertip. This is a small area and precision is important to get the best results when treating pain in the head, eyes, nose, ears, sinuses, mouth, and chin.

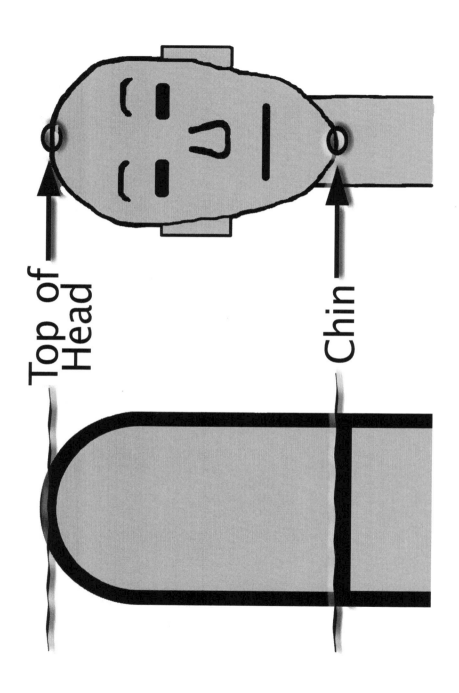

On the palm side of the tip of the middle finger, the entire face is represented. The top of the head is a couple of millimeters in front of the underside of the fingernail. The chin is at the group of creases on the first joint. The area between these two points represents the face or front of the head.

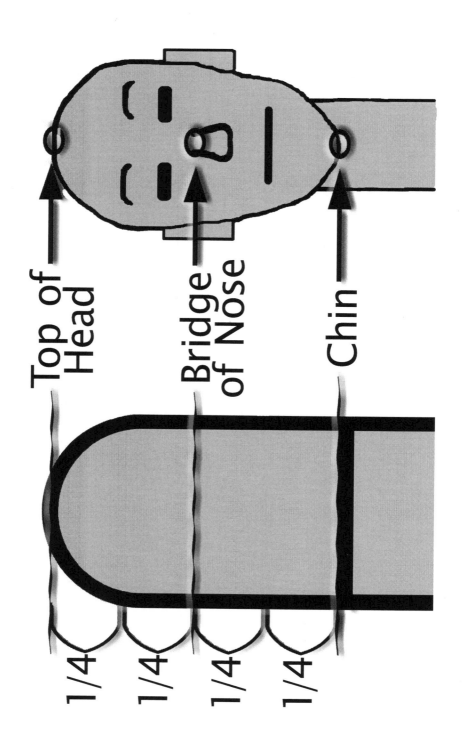

Looking at the tip of the middle finger, figure out where the halfway point is between the tip of the finger and the group of creases at the first joint. This point represents the bridge of the nose. This is where glasses sit on your nose or where the bones of the skull end and the cartilage of the nose begins. It is important to remember that this point does NOT represent the tip of the nose. Correctly identifying the bridge of the nose is important for locating where the eyes and other parts of the face are represented on the finger.

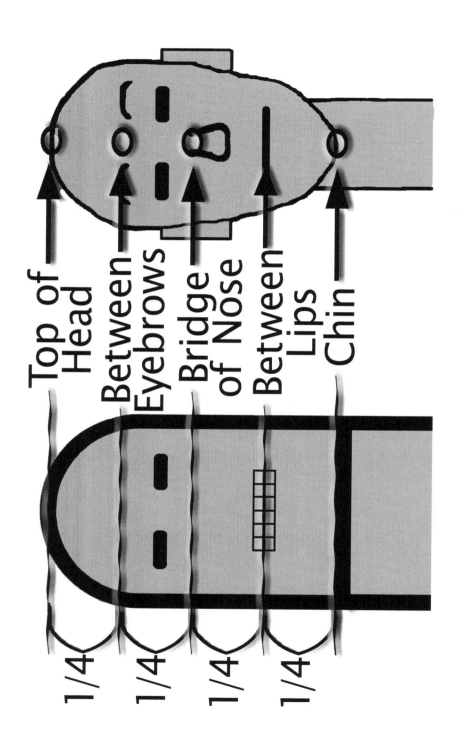

Top of Head

Between Eyebrows

Bridge of Nose

Between Lips

Chin

1/4

1/4

1/4

1/4

Divide the area between the top of the head and the bridge of the nose in half. This is one quarter of the way down the midline of the fingertip and represents the space between the eyebrows. Some people also refer to this area as the "third eye" and it is an important landmark for key features of the face.

The forehead is in the top one quarter of the tip of the middle finger. The frontal sinuses are also in this area, slightly above each eyebrow.

The eyes are in the second quarter of the tip of the finger, between the eyebrows and the bridge of the nose, on either side of the midline. The maxillary sinuses are in this area as well, below each eye.

Because these are common locations of pain associated with headaches, it is important to know the corresponding locations on the tip of the middle finger. Take a moment to review the diagram to make sure you understand the location of the eyes on the palm side of the middle fingertip.

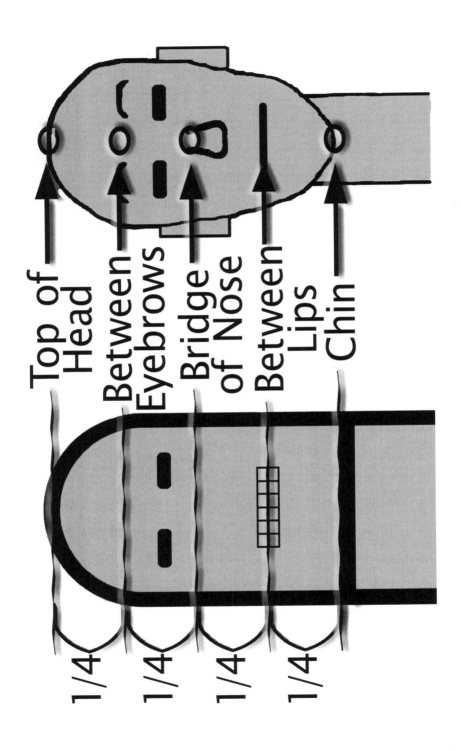

Divide the area between the bridge of the nose and the chin in half. This is three quarters of the way down the middle fingertip and represents the space between the upper lip and the lower lip. This point also marks the division between the mandible and jaw, if you imagine extending it around the sides of the face. The upper lips, teeth and gums are right above the three quarter mark. The lower lips, teeth, and gums are right below the three quarter mark.

Just as your ears are located on the sides of your head, the ears are represented on both sides of the tip of the middle finger. The temporomandibular joint (TMJ) is represented on both sides at the finger, slightly in front of where the ear lobes would be.

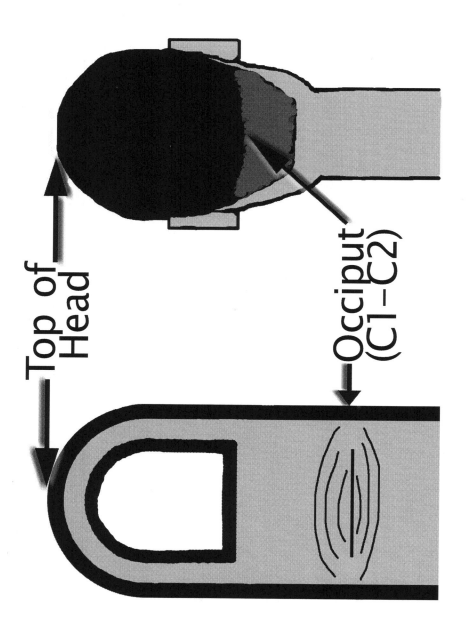

Top of Head

Occiput (C1–C2)

The back side of the middle fingertip, from the top of the finger to the group of creases at the first joint, represents the back of the head. The top part of the back of the middle finger is covered by the fingernail, which makes this area not accessible for treatment. If there is pain in this area of your head, the search for corresponding tender points must be done in the surrounding areas below the nail or on the sides of the nail. There also might be tender points on the upper part of the palm side of the middle finger, even if you do not have pain in the forehead or around the eyes that are represented in that location.

Most people have tender points above and below the first joint on the back of the middle finger, even if they do not complain of pain in the corresponding parts of the body - the occiput of their head or the upper part of the back of their neck. The muscles on the back of the neck attach here and there is always muscle tension in this area from supporting the head. If you have a headache or neck pain, an additional search in this area will show tender points that will produce better results than if you limit your search to only where you feel the pain.

Notes:_____

_____

_____

_____

_____

_____

_____

_____

_____

_____

_____

_____

_____

_____

_____

_____

_____

_____

_____

_____

_____

_____

_____

_____

_____

_____

_____

_____

_____

_____

_____

_____

_____

_____

_____

_____

Arms

We will use the left hand as an example in this chapter, but remember that both arms are projected onto each hand. To locate the arms on the hand, start with the hand in the crawling animal/crouching man position for the quickest and easiest way to avoid finger confusion. Notice that the arms are clearly represented on the hand by the ring and index fingers.

Because we will focus on the three outer fingers and use the hand on the same side as where the pain is in the body, we will use the ring finger on the left hand, which represents the left arm on the body. The index finger on the left hand represents the right arm of the body, but for the most effective results in treating right arm pain it would be best to use the ring finger on the right hand.

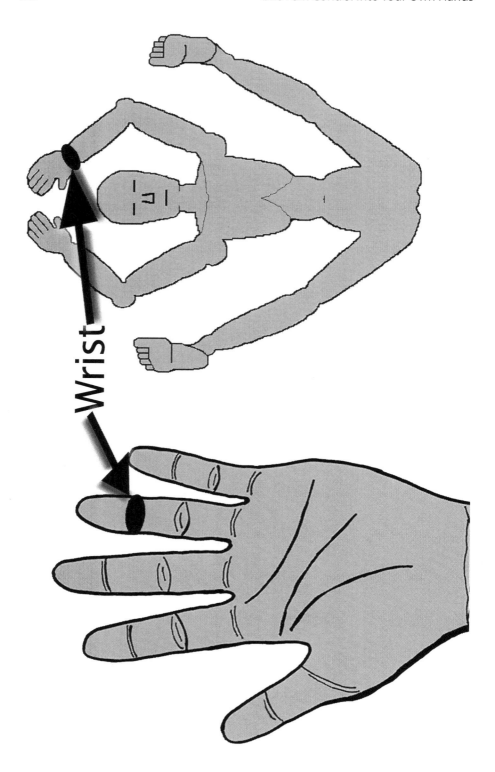

Look at your left hand, palm side up with the fingers held upright. The front of the left arm on the body is represented on the palm side of the left ring finger.

With the hand held upright, the first joint on the ring finger represents the wrist joint. On the palm side of the hand, you will see a few creases close together in this area, but the most prominent grouping of creases is the landmark of the wrist joint. The palm side of the hand and fingers on the body are represented on the palm side of the fingertip of the ring finger, from the top of the finger to the first joint.

The thumb is represented on the medial side of the tip of the ring finger (on the side closest to the middle finger). This is similar to how your thumb would be next to your head if you raise your arms up alongside your head. The pinky finger on the body is represented on the lateral side of the tip of the ring finger (on the side closest to the pinky finger).

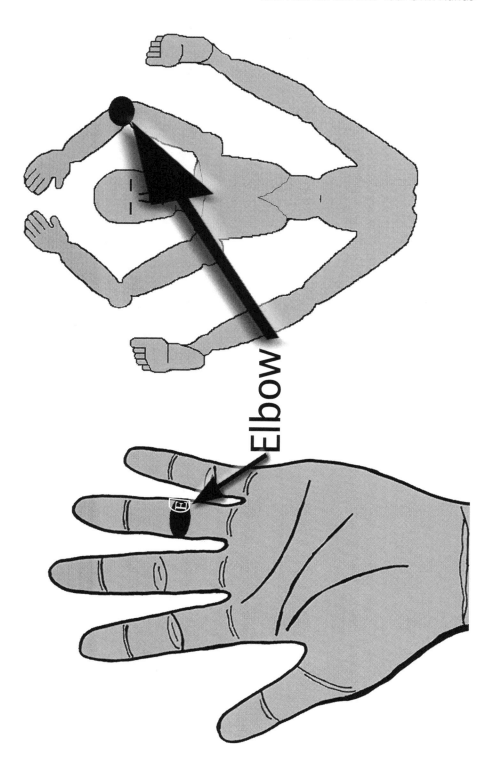

Elbow

With the hand held upright, the second joint on the palm side of the ring finger represents the front side of the elbow joint. This area usually has several creases that are spread apart, but the lowest group of creases are the landmark of the elbow joint.

The bony part of the elbow is located on the lateral side of the ring finger, on the side closest to the pinky finger. This is because it is neither on the front nor the back of our bodies. Half of the bony part of the elbow is on the front of the body and half is on the back of the body. Raising your arm alongside your head makes this more clear. Notice that your elbow points outward on the side of the arms opposite your head and is NOT in the center of the back of the arm.

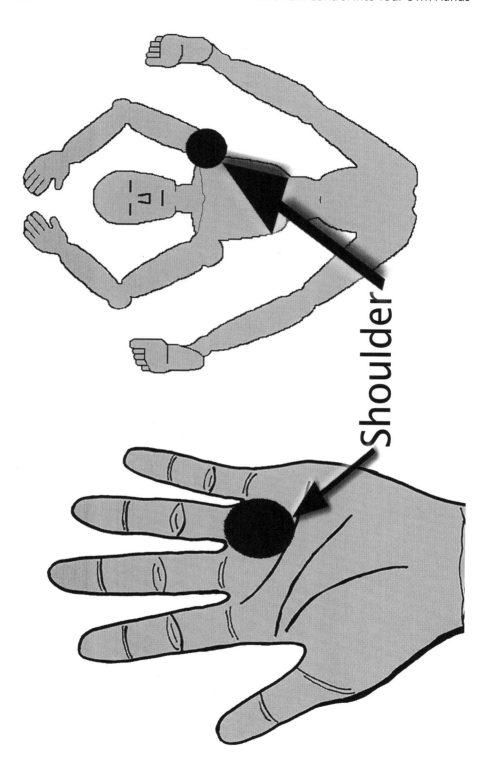

Shoulder

Look at the palm side of the left ring finger on your upright hand. The third joint is not where you might think it
is. The first two joints were easy to locate by looking for the
creases on the finger. But the third crease from the top,
where the finger meets the palm, is NOT a joint. Instead,
the third joint is located in the upper palm, between where
the ring finger attaches to the palm and the crease that
runs across your palm (under the pinky, ring and middle
fingers). To confirm this, put the thumb from your opposite
hand under the ring finger and your index finger from the
opposite hand on the ring finger's knuckle on the back of
the hand. Now wiggle your ring finger back and forth and
notice that the movement comes from this area, which represents the front of the shoulder joint.

Because the shoulder joint area is large, it takes longer to
find the corresponding points to treat shoulder pain than it
does to search for points in most other areas of the hand.
For the best results when treating shoulder pain, take the
time needed to do a thorough search of this area to locate
all the points.

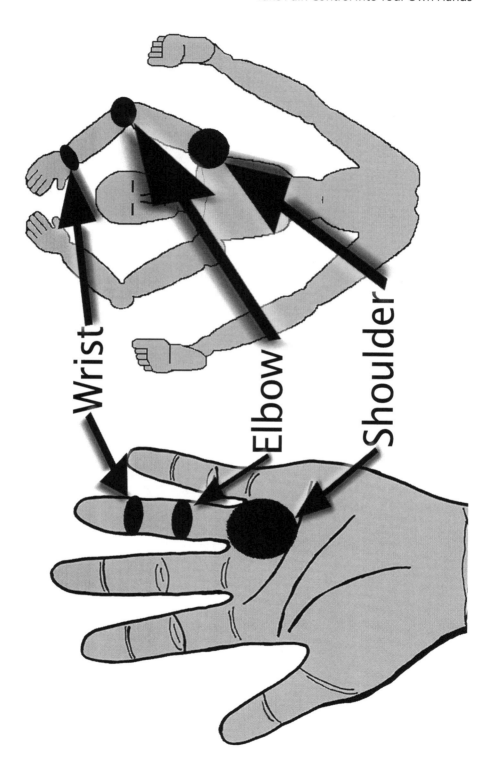

Think about how the palm side of the left ring finger represents the front of the left arm on the body. If you were to raise your arm alongside your head, the sequence of joints from top to bottom - wrist, elbow, shoulder - would perfectly match how they are represented on the ring finger with the hand held upright.

Although we are focusing on the left ring finger as a representation of the left arm, remember that the right arm is also represented as the index finger on the left hand. To better visualize this, make the crawling animal/crouching man figure with your hand to see that the index and ring fingers are the arms.

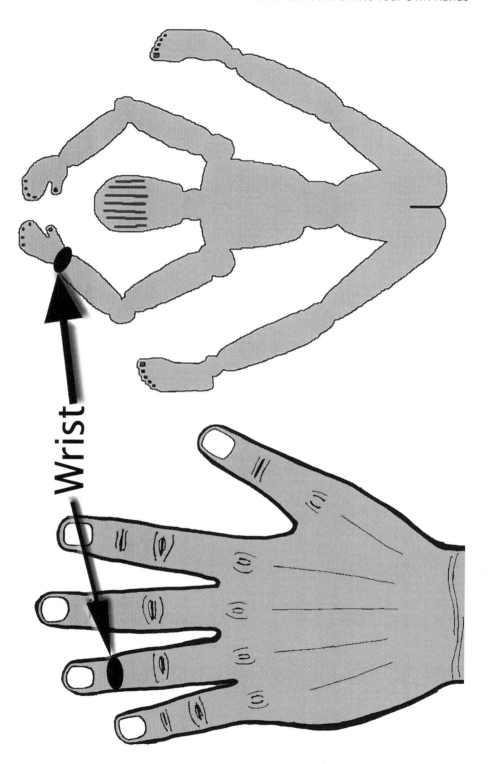

Wrist

Now turn your left hand over and look at the back of your hand. The back of the left arm on the body is represented on the back of the left ring finger.

On the back of the hand, the center of the group of creases on the first joint represents the wrist joint. The area from the tip of the ring finger to the first joint represents the back side of the hand. Much of the area above the joint, corresponding to the back of the fingers, is covered by the nail. Because you cannot poke on the fingernail, pain located on the back of the hand on the body is treated around the fingernail or on the palm side of the ring finger.

The thumb on the body is represented on the medial side of the tip of the ring finger (on the side of the ring finger closest to the middle finger). This is similar to how your thumb would be next to your head if you raise your arms and legs up towards your head. Similarly the pinky finger on the body is represented on the lateral side of the tip of the ring finger (on the side closest to the pinky finger).

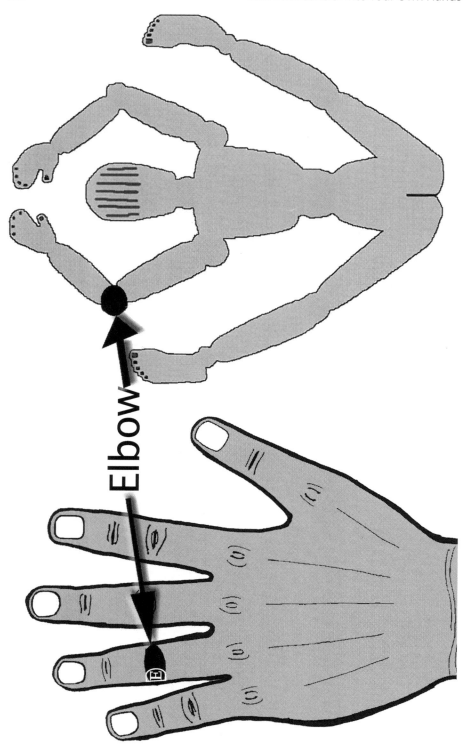

Elbow

On the back side of the hand, the center of the group of creases on the second joint represents the elbow joint. The back side of the bony part of the elbow is located on the outer edge of the ring finger, on the side closest to the pinky finger. It sticks out to the side when the arm is raised above your head and the corresponding area on the finger is located in this same spot.

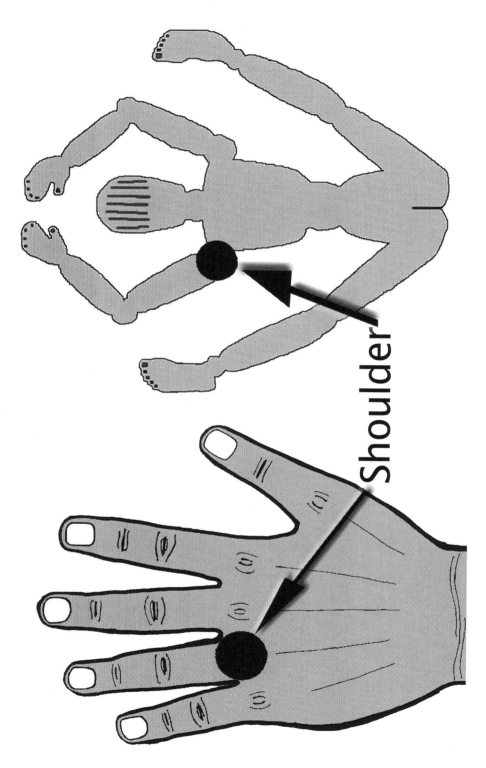

The back of the shoulder joint is represented on the back of the ring finger at the knuckle joint. The size of the shoulder joint on the hand is larger than the size of the elbow or wrist joints. It starts where the ring finger attaches to the hand and ends at the bottom of the knuckle.

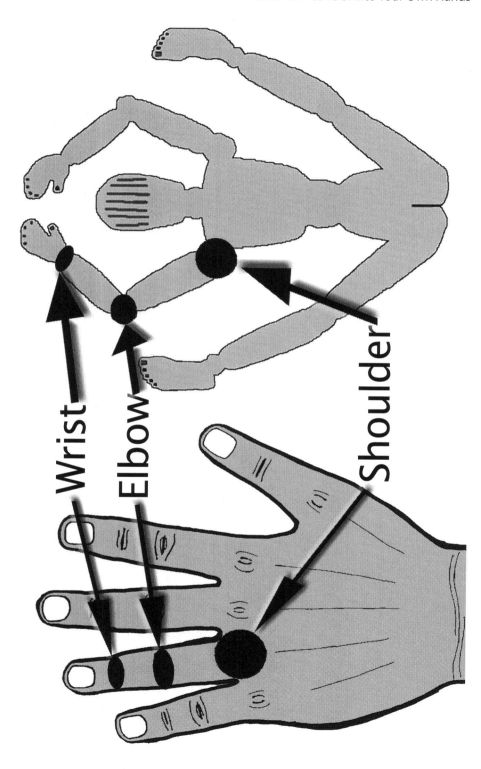

Looking at the ring finger on the back of the hand, it is again easy to see how it represents an arm raised alongside the head. With the hand held upright, the sequence of joints from top to bottom - wrist, elbow, shoulder - is the same.

Although we are focusing on the left ring finger as a representation of the left arm, remember that the right arm is also represented as the index finger on the left hand. To better visualize this, make the crawling animal/crouching man figure with your hand to see that the index and ring fingers are the arms.

Notes:_____

Legs

For simplicity, we will use the left hand as an example in this chapter but remember that both legs are projected onto each hand. To locate the legs on the hand, start with the hand in the crawling animal/crouching man position for the quickest and easiest way to avoid finger confusion. Notice that the legs are clearly represented on the hand by the pinky finger and thumb.

Because we are going to focus on the three outer fingers and use the hand on the same side as where the pain is in the body, we will use the pinky finger on the left hand, which represents the left leg on the body. The thumb on the left hand represents the right leg of the body, but for the most effective results in treating right leg pain it would be best to use the pinky finger on the right hand.

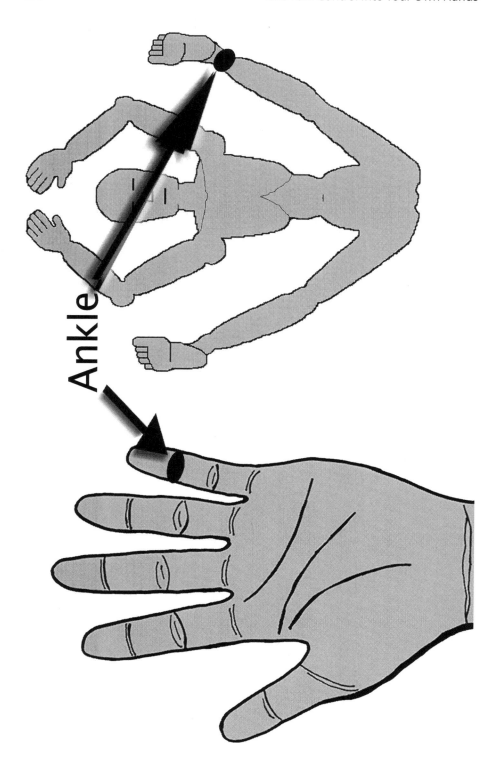

Ankle

Look at your left hand, palm side up with the fingers held upright. The front of the left leg on the body is represented on the palm side of the left pinky finger.

With the hand held upright, the first joint on the pinky finger represents the ankle joint. On the palm side of the hand, you will see a few creases close together in this area. The most prominent grouping of creases is the landmark of the ankle joint. The sole of the foot and toes on the body are represented on the palm side of the fingertip of the pinky finger, from the top of the finger to the first joint.

The big toe is represented on the medial side of the tip of the pinky finger (on the side closest to the ring finger). This is similar to how your big toe would be next to your arm if you raised your arms and legs up alongside your head. Similarly, the pinky toe on the body is represented on the lateral side of the tip of the pinky finger (on the outer edge of the pinky finger).

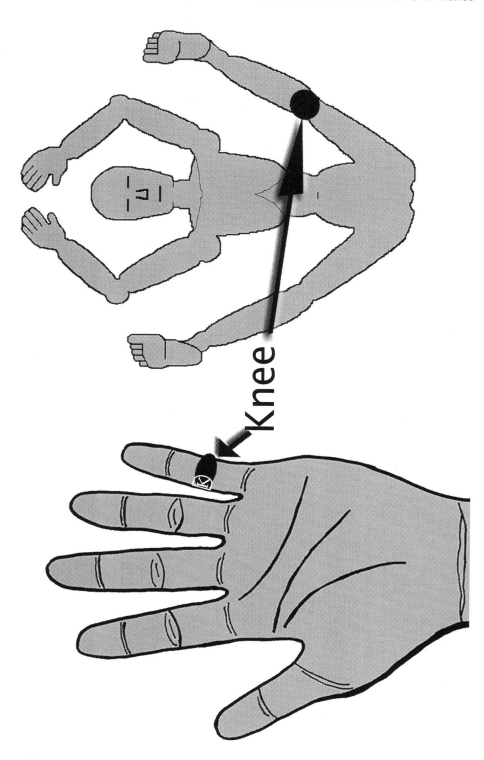

Knee

With the hand held upright, the second joint on the palm side of the pinky finger represents the front side of the knee joint. This area usually has several creases that are spread apart, but the lowest group of creases are the landmark of the knee joint.

The kneecap is located on the medial side of the pinky finger, on the side closest to the ring finger. This is because it is neither on the front nor the back of our bodies. Half of the kneecap is on the front of the body and half is on the back of the body. Raising your leg alongside your head or standing with your feet angled out to the sides makes this more clear. Notice that your kneecap points towards your head on the side of the raised leg and it is NOT in the center of the front of the leg.

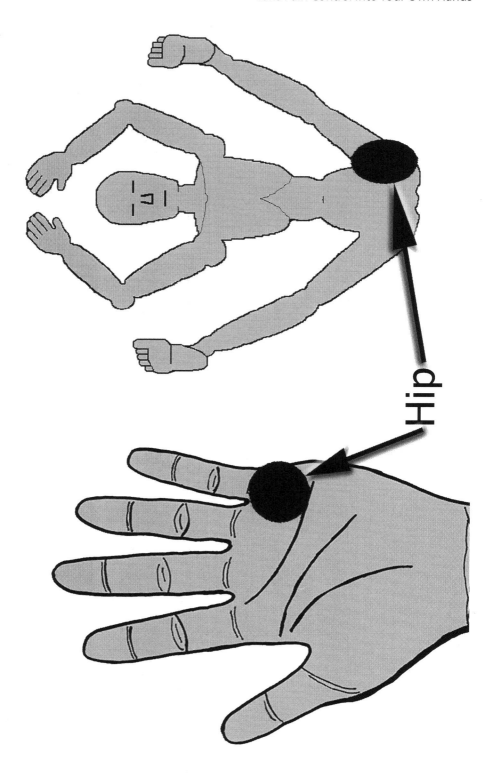

Hip

Look at the palm side of the pinky finger on your upright hand. The third joint is not where you might think it is. The first two joints were easy to locate by looking for the creases on the finger. But the third crease from the top, where the finger meets the palm, is NOT a joint. Instead, the third joint is located in the upper palm, between where the pinky finger attaches to the palm and the crease that runs across your palm (under the pinky, ring and middle fingers). To confirm this, put the thumb from your opposite hand under the pinky finger and your index finger from the opposite hand on the pinky finger's knuckle on the back of the hand. Now wiggle your pinky finger back and forth and notice that the movement comes from this area, which represents the front of the hip joint.

Because the hip joint area is large, it takes longer to find the corresponding points to treat hip pain than it does to search for points in most other areas of the hand. For the best results when treating hip pain, take the time needed to do a thorough search of this area to locate all the points.

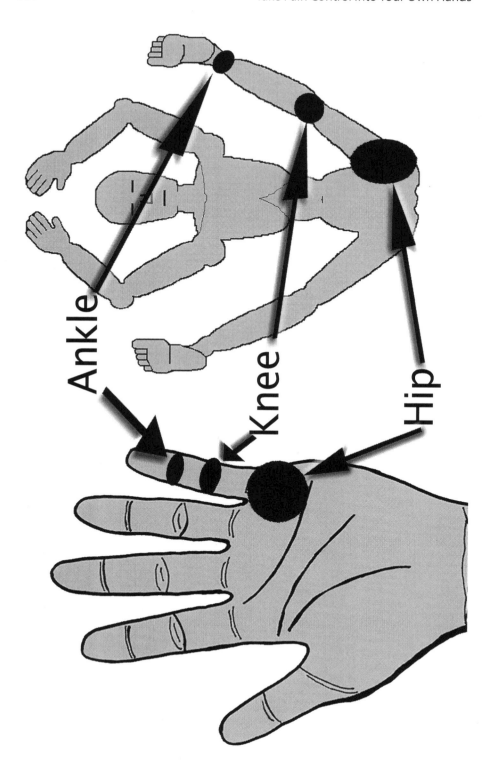

Think about how the palm side of the left pinky finger represents the front of the leg on the body. If you were to raise your leg alongside your head, the sequence of joints from top to bottom - ankle, knee, hip - would perfectly match how they are represented on the pinky finger with the hand held upright.

Although we are focusing on the left pinky finger as a representation of the left leg, remember that the right leg is also represented as the thumb on the left hand. To better visualize this, make the crawling animal/crouching man figure with your hand to see that the thumb and pinky fingers are the legs.

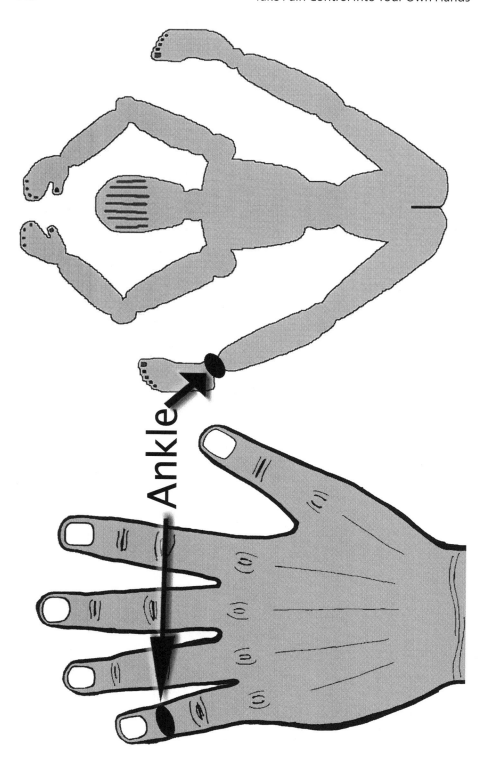

Ankle

Now turn your hand over and look at the back of your hand. The back of the left leg on the body is represented on the back of the left pinky finger.

On the back of the hand, the center of the group of creases on the first joint represents the ankle joint. The area from the tip of the pinky finger to the first joint represents the back side of the foot. Much of the area above the joint, corresponding to the back of the fingers, is covered by the nail. Because you can't poke on the fingernail, pain located on the back of the foot on the body is treated around the fingernail or on the palm side of the pinky finger, where the sole is represented.

The big toe on the body is represented on the medial side of the tip of the pinky finger (on the side of the pinky finger closest to the ring finger). This is similar to how your big toe would be next to your arm if you raise your arms and legs up towards your head. Similarly, the pinky toe on the body is represented on the lateral side of the pinky finger's fingertip (on the outer edge of the pinky finger).

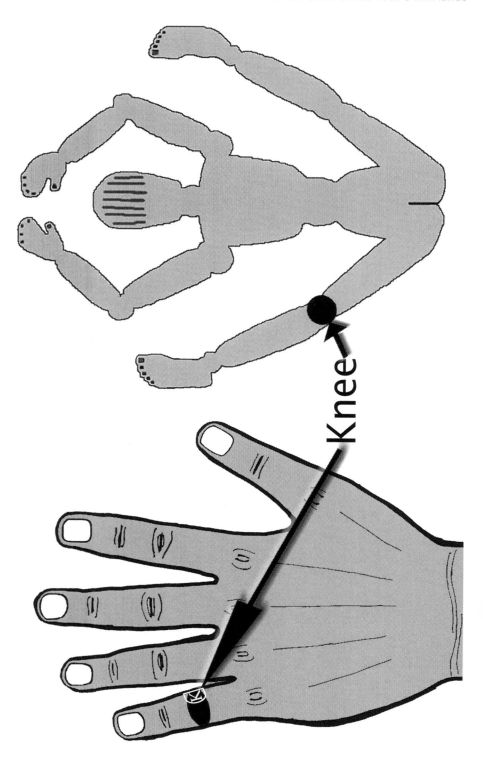

Knee

On the back side of the hand, the center of the group of creases on the second joint represents the knee joint. The back side of the kneecap is located on the inner edge of the pinky finger, on the side closest to the ring finger. The knee sticks out to the side if you stand with your feet angled outward or if your legs were raised alongside your head. The corresponding area on the finger is located in this same spot.

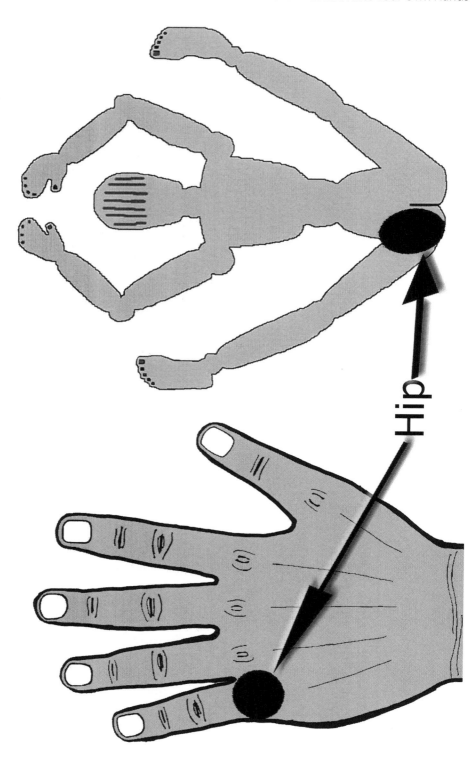

Hip

The back of the hip joint is represented on the back of the pinky finger at the knuckle joint. The size of the hip joint on the hand is larger than the size of the knee or ankle joints. It starts where the pinky finger attaches to the hand and ends at the bottom of the knuckle.

Remember that I said we would not be using the thumb unless absolutely necessary? The reason for this is clear when we try to find the representation of the hip joint on the thumb. Go ahead and try for yourself. The first joint is the ankle, the second joint is the knee, and the third joint is... missing? Actually, the third joint of the thumb is way down by where the index finger meets the wrist. It can be difficult to locate because it is buried deep under muscle.

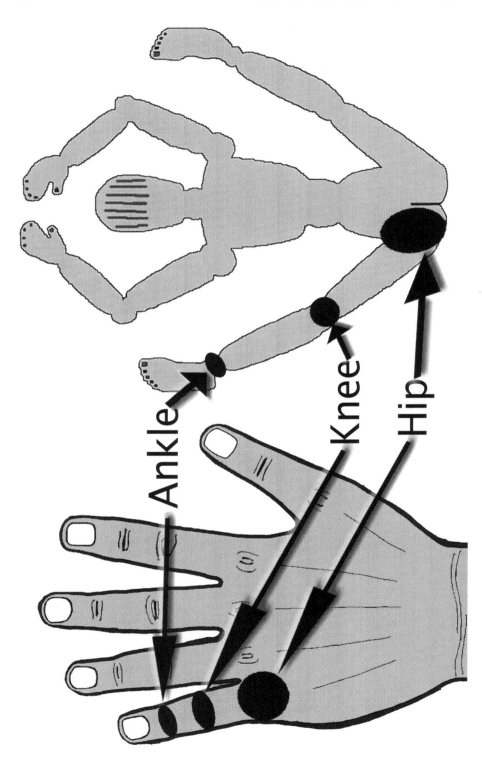

Looking at the pinky finger on the back of the hand, it is again easy to see how it represents a leg raised up toward the head. With the hand held upright, the sequence of joints from top to bottom - ankle, knee, hip - is the same.

Although we are focusing on the left pinky finger as a representation of the left leg, remember that the right leg is also represented as the thumb on the left hand. To better visualize this, make the crawling animal/crouching man figure with your hand to see that the thumb and pinky fingers are the legs.

Notes:_____

Locating Points on the Hands

Precisely locating discrete points on the hands is the key to using Correspondence Korean Hand Therapy to manage your own pain. Tender points are often located millimeters away from nontender points, so accuracy makes a big difference in getting the maximum benefit from using this system.

An important step before searching for points is to rub your hands together. This stimulates the hands and makes it easier to locate the active points. If your hands tend to be cold or if you have poor circulation in your hands, this step is especially important. Korean Hand Therapy rollers can be used to stimulate the hands with bumpy projections for a deeper stimulation, but I have found that vigorously rubbing the hands together works just as well. Make sure to rub both the palm and back surfaces of the hands before beginning.

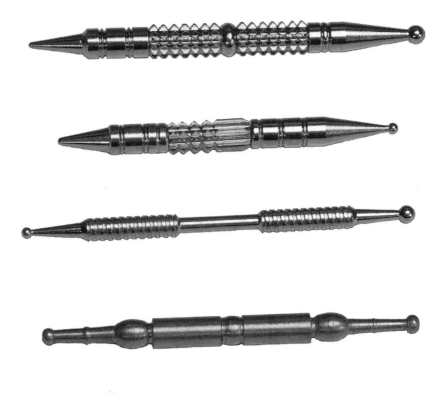

Tools to Locate Hand Points

Treatment points are located using a blunt-tipped metal probe that is tapered like a pen or has a small ball at one or both ends. Some have large and small ends for both general and precise searches. Others have one or more rollers with spiky projections on their shafts, allowing stimulation of several points at once. Specially designed tools for this purpose can be purchased from stores that sell Korean Hand Therapy supplies. Most acupuncture supply stores do not sell them and hand probes are shorter than the long metal probes typically used for ear acupuncture or auriculotherapy.

If you do not have a special tool, you can still locate and stimulate points on the hands effectively with a ballpoint pen that has run out of ink. A working ballpoint pen is less ideal because the ink leaves marks everywhere when you press it onto your skin, making it hard to distinguish non-active points from active ones. Dental probes can be used but only the ones with rounded tips, not the sharp ones used to scrape teeth. Many hobby stores also sell metal tipped tools with small balls on the ends.

You will also need a thin marker or felt-tipped pen to mark the active points that need to be stimulated. Any pen marker will do but darker colors are easier to see on the skin. Permanent markers are best because they are less likely to rub off. (Don't worry - permanent markers are not permanent on your skin.) I prefer surgical markers because the ink lasts longer and will usually make it through a few hand washings. I have also had good results with the markers tattoo artists to use to draw designs on the skin.

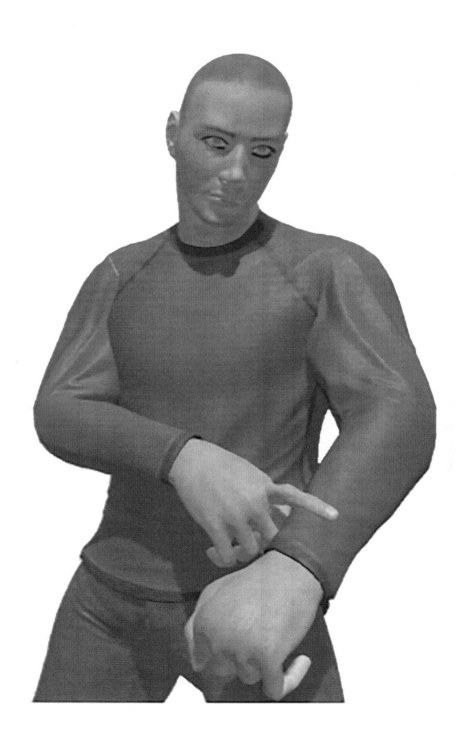

First, Focus on Pain in the Body

Before searching for points on the hand, it is important to first assess the painful area of the body you want to treat. If you do not have pain now, there is no way you will be able to know if Correspondence Korean Hand Therapy has helped you. You would not take a dose of pain medication for a headache when you do not have a headache, right? Therefore, wait until you experience the pain before using this system to relieve it.

If there is a particular movement that intensifies the pain in your body, it is important to do that before you begin. You may need to bend or twist your back, flex or extend your arm or leg, push on the sore spots of your head, or turn your neck to better locate the pain. The more accurately you locate the pain on your body, the easier it will be to narrow the search area on your hand and the more effective the treatment will be. Provoking the pain in your body will also make the corresponding points in your hands more tender and easier to find.

Assess the pain intensity by giving it a score from zero to ten. This will make it easier for you to evaluate the improvement after you use Correspondence Korean Hand Therapy to treat the pain.

Find the specific location of the pain on the body that you want to treat. If you can, point to the painful area on the body with one finger to better localize it. Is it on the left or right of side of your body? Is it on the front or back of your body? What key landmarks on the body are on either side of the pain location?

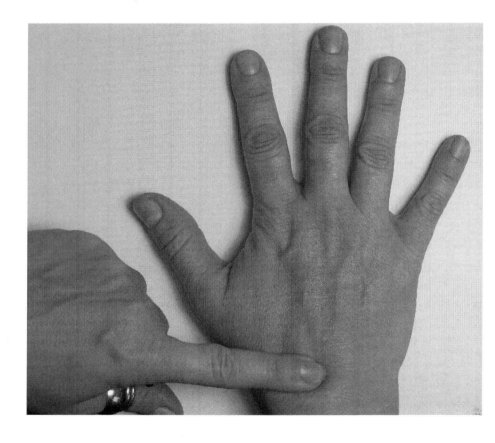

Determine The Search Location on the Hand

Use what you previously learned about the map of the body on the hands to decide if you should use the right or left hand. Then, figure out if you should use the palm side or back side of that hand. Finally, locate the key landmarks on the hand that correspond to the landmarks on the body closest to the location of the pain. The area between the landmarks on the hand is your search zone.

This is a critical step because searching the wrong area of the hand will locate tender points that are unrelated to your pain and result in an ineffective treatment. A good analogy is the hunt for the missing Malaysia Airlines plane. A search of the entire ocean will likely locate interesting things underwater that are unrelated to the crash. It would take hundreds of years to complete the search if it were done without limiting the search area based on the plane's last known location. If you get confused, stop and return to the location of the pain in your body to be sure that you find the right search zone on the hand before starting the precision search for treatment points.

Begin with a general search of the hand in the area between the landmarks, using a finger with firm pressure to see if you can find a smaller area that is uncomfortable when pressure is applied. You might notice that such areas on the hand also feel different, kind of lumpy or crunchy under the skin. If you have a hand probe with a large ball on one end, you can drag it across the skin with a little pressure. If the search zone is on a finger, you can roll the shaft of a pen along the finger while applying pressure.

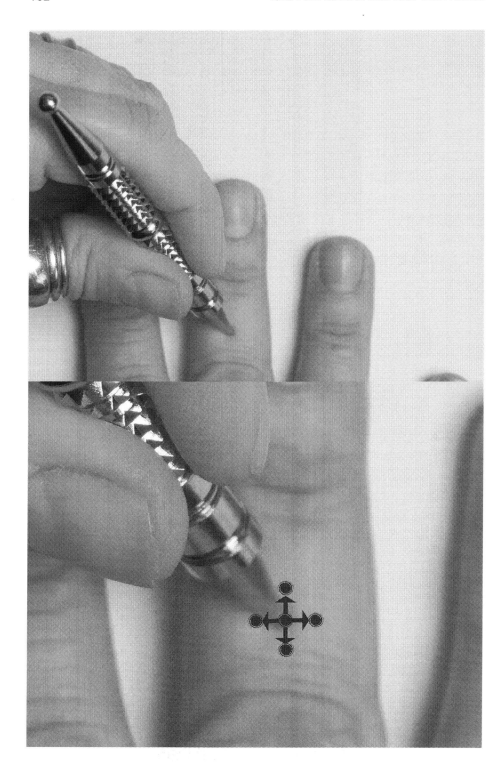

Precision Search for Active Points

The most efficient way to perform the detailed search is to use a grid-like pattern, checking points a few millimeters apart. Try making a straight line while searching so you do not miss any part of the search zone. Stop and mark each active point as you find them. When I find an active point, I always search above, below, to the right and to the left of it because painful points tend appear in clusters in a particular area. The search areas corresponding to joints in the arms and legs are especially large and will require more time to locate all the active points. Where we feel the pain in a joint is often not the same place where there is an injury in the joint. Doing a thorough search of joint areas will identify more active points and will result in a more effective reduction in pain.

When searching for points, use about the same amount of pressure as you use with a pen when you write on paper. People are usually surprised at how little pressure is needed to find the points. The goal is not to damage or puncture the skin, but rather to determine if a point is sensitive to pressure or not. When you feel discomfort at a particular point, stop pressing, mark it with the marker, and continue searching for other points above or below it.

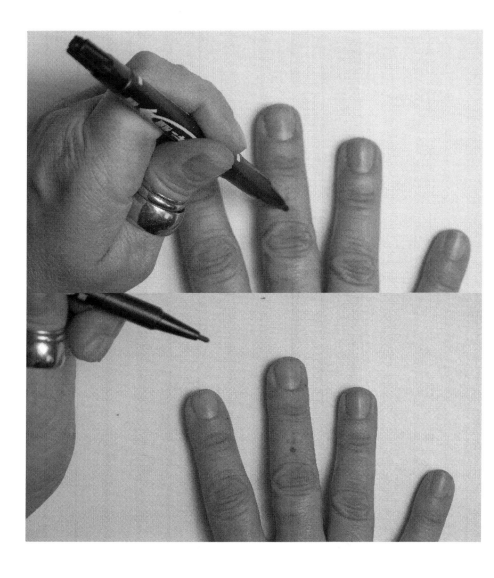

Active points on the hand are tender to pressure. In some people, they are extremely tender and may feel like a sharp, stabbing pain or burning sensation when pressure is applied. In people with higher pain tolerances, the points may not be painful but usually feel different or somewhat more uncomfortable than when the same pressure is applied to other areas of the hand. In general, the more tender the point, the more active it is and the more it needs to be treated. When you are looking for active points, the goal is to find all the points that need to be treated. Do not compare points or try to analyze if one point is more tender than another. Ask yourself if each point is tender or not, considering it as a yes or no question. Sometimes points that were not tender at first may feel tender if you go back and check again later. If this happens, mark it as a tender point and continue with your search.

You may notice that after you find a tender point, the skin in that spot may appear somewhat dark or purplish. This is a confirmation that this point indeed needs to be treated. According to Traditional Chinese Medicine, this would be interpreted as stagnation of blood or energy flow in the area. This discoloration is especially helpful in people with high pain tolerances who may not feel much difference between active and non-active points. It also helps make it easier to find the point if you happen to look away for a second when reaching for your marker.

Mark each point carefully as soon as you identify it as an active point. Once all the tender points are marked in the search area, it is time to stimulate the points to treat your pain.

Notes:_____

_____
_____
_____
_____
_____
_____
_____
_____
_____
_____
_____
_____
_____
_____
_____
_____
_____
_____
_____
_____
_____
_____
_____
_____
_____
_____
_____
_____
_____
_____
_____

Activating Points on the Hands

Once you have identified several tender points on the hands with a thorough search, it is time to activate them to reduce your pain. This is the easiest part of the process.

Look at the points you have marked on your hand. Place the tip of your probe or ballpoint pen carefully on one mark. Apply pressure with just a little wiggle until it hurts and move on, doing the same thing to each marked point. You need to apply the same pressure on each mark that you used to find each point. When you have stimulated all the points, repeat the process of brief stimulation of each point two more times, for a total of three rounds on all points. Remember, you are not trying to damage the skin with too much pressure. Stop as soon as you feel any discomfort and move on to the next point right away.

When you are done, recheck the part of the body that is painful. Repeat the body movements you did before searching for the points on your hand to compare how your body feels now.

- Do you notice an increase in the range of motion of the part of the body?

- Did the pain improve or stay the same?

- Did the pain move or stay in the same location?

If the pain in your body improved but is still present in the same location, repeat two or three rounds of stimulating all the points again to see if the pain continues to improve.

If the pain in your body is unchanged, recheck your point location.

- Are you on the correct hand and finger?

- Are you on the correct side of the hand that represents the side of the body with pain?

- Are you searching in the correct search zone based on the landmarks of the hand? It is easy to get mixed up and search the wrong area on the hands when you first use this system. This is the most common reason for not getting pain-relieving results when using Correspondence Korean Hand Therapy.

  - If you miscalculated and searched the wrong area, reorient yourself again to the map of the body on the hands and do a new search in the correct area.

  - If you are confident that you found the correct search area the first time, repeat a search in the same zone. There will often be points that were not tender during the first search that are tender the second time around.

If the pain in your body moved, you will need to search the new area on the hand that corresponds to the area of the body where the pain has moved to. The pain did not actually move, but it can feel like it did. There are often multiple areas of pain in the body at once, but we focus on the most severe one. You did not notice the secondary areas of pain until you relieved the pain in the primary area that was masking it. Treating pain is like peeling back the layers of an onion to reveal what is underneath each one.

- Once the second search is done with the additional points identified and marked, do another two to three rounds of stimulating all the points. Move your body again to confirm that the main pain site is still improved and the secondary pain site is now better.

I always recommend people take a photograph of the marked points after achieving pain relief. Do this right away, before you wash the marks off or smear them. If the pain returns, the points that need to be retreated in the hand will be in the same place. A photograph will help you quickly find the points again without having to do another detailed search. Most cell phones have a camera and having a photograph of the points with you whereever you go will remind you to stimulate the points again.

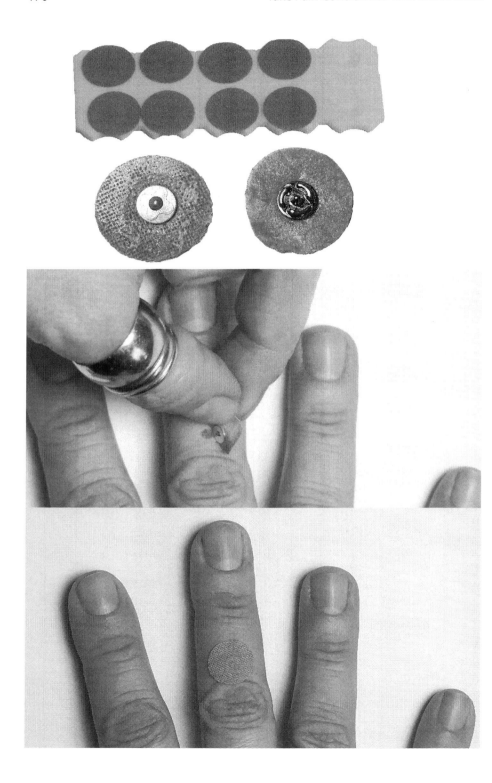

Press Pellets

Pressing the active points on the hands is the quickest and easiest way to reduce acute pain. For chronic pain conditions, prolonged stimulation of the points that need frequent treatment can be beneficial and will produce longer lasting results.

Korean Hand Therapy press pellets are flat, metal discs with a protrusion on a round adhesive bandage. The protruding part is carefully placed onto the tender points for continued stimulation. Larger discs with multiple projections are also available to treat large areas with multiple active points. Individual pellets can be carefully repositioned on the adhesive bandages if you want to treat a group of points that are close together. After application, they can be left alone or gentle pressure can be applied with a finger every few hours to intensify the stimulation. Applying medical tape on top of the adhesive discs helps keep them in place.

Press pellets are most often used overnight because they tend to fall off the hands due to perspiration, hand washing, and normal daily activities. They are best left on for at least six hours but should be removed after twenty four hours to allow the skin to breathe. The pellets can be re-used several times, as long as the metal on the disc remains shiny. Avoiding the use of hand lotions with press pellets will make them last longer.

Press pellets are especially useful for prolonged treatment of low back pain because of its chronic nature. They are also a great treatment option for kids, elderly people with fragile skin on their hands, or anyone who is sensitive to pain and does not like poking on themselves.

Press pellets come in two colors - silver (made of aluminum) or gold (made of brass with a gold coating). According to principles of Traditional Chinese Medicine, metals have a bioelectric effect so the use of press pellets has this added benefit in addition to continuously stimulating the points. Colorless metals (silver, white gold, aluminum) reduce excess conditions and colored metals (yellow or rose gold, brass, bronze) are stimulating. Because pain is considered an excess condition, silver press pellets are preferred for the treatment of pain. Gold press pellets can also treat pain if silver is not available, but the two metal colors should not be used together in Correspondence Korean Hand Therapy treatments.

Manual Massage

Massage is an easy way to treat your pain as you can do it anywhere, anytime, and without anyone knowing what you are doing. It can be done while you are talking on the phone, sitting in a class or conference, or even under a table at a meal. Rubbing your hands together is a natural activity and people will just think your hands are sore or cold.

When you massage your own hands, you are essentially giving yourself a full body massage. Pay special attention to areas on the hands that correspond to problems in the body to maximize the benefit. Lots of pressure with your thumb or pinching the area can help treat tender spots that need deeper stimulation. Pressing your fingernails into the skin is a great way to stimulate points when you are in pain and do not have a pen or any other tools around. Use just enough pressure to make the points hurt a little and quickly move on to another area to avoid accidentally cutting your skin with sharp nails.

Rolling Massage

Some Korean Hand Therapy probes have the added feature of one or more rollers with little spikes that rotate around the center shaft. This is an easy way to provide deep stimulation to large areas of the hands where there are several active points.

You can roll the side of a pen or a probe with a smooth shaft up and down a finger while applying pressure to stimulate several points at the same time. This technique can also help narrow down a search area on a finger, because the discrete tender points are easily located in the area that is tender when the pen rolls across it.

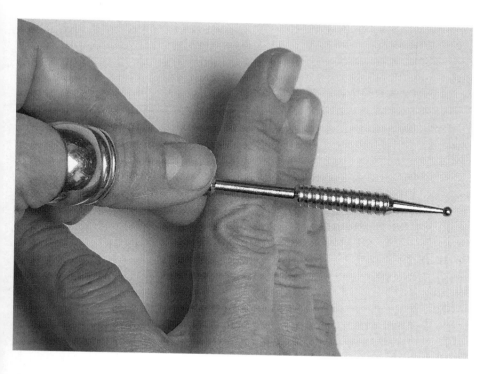

Magnet Therapy

Small hand magnets can be taped to the skin for strong stimulation of active points on the hands. Magnets are applied to the body with the north pole contacting the skin, which has a reducing effect to treat pain. Most acupuncture therapy magnets sold on tapes are set up in this orientation. Loose magnets may have a small indentation on the north pole side. Use of magnets in young children who might swallow them should be avoided because swallowed magnets can attract each other and pinch areas of the intestines together, causing dangerous blockages.

How Often Should I Stimulate the Points?

The simple answer to this question is to stimulate the points again whenever the pain returns. Pain medications can improve pain but when their effect wears off, the pain may return. This does not mean that pain medication does not work, but rather that the underlying problem persists. Acute pain, like a headache or minor injury may only require a single treatment with Correspondence Korean Hand Therapy but chronic pain will almost always require repeat treatments. The good news is that with repeated stimulation of points on the hands, people often notice that the effects last longer and less frequent treatments are needed as time goes on.

According to Korean Hand Therapy principles, as long as the corresponding points in your hand are tender, they need additional treatment. If the pain in your body significantly improved or even if the pain has completely disappeared, tender points that remain in the corresponding area of the hand indicate that the problem requires more treatment. Perhaps the pain level in your body has dropped so significantly that it you no longer notice it. If the points on your hands are still tender, the pain may return and it is best to stimulate the points intermittently to help prolong the pain relief you have achieved.

Consider using press pellets at night to treat chronic conditions in order to reduce daytime discomfort. I do not usually recommend people wear press pellets on palm points during the day because they fall off easily with hand washing and normal daytime activities, even with the use of additional tape.

Other Ways to Activate Points on the Hands

Once you have identified the points on the hands that correspond to pain in your body, there are several ways to use them to improve your pain. Methods of stimulation that cause a bit of discomfort result in faster improvements in pain and range of motion. Stimulation that targets the points without discomfort does not usually result in the same immediate pain relief, but can promote more subtle, long-term benefits.

Many people who use Korean Hand Therapy have experience with other treatment modalities to manage their pain. These treatments can be integrated with Correspondence Korean Hand Therapy points in creative ways. Once you accurately identify the points on the hand that correspond to pain in your body, the treatment options are unlimited.

Electrical Stimulation

Electrical stimulation devices are commonly used in various types of acupuncture. Electrical current is used to stimulate points and the results can be as effective as needles or blunt pressure on Korean Hand Therapy Points. The intensity of the current can be changed to make treatment more comfortable. Many of these devices have pen-shaped tips that can be used to treat small areas. Some of these devices have the added feature of being able to detect active acupuncture points by measuring decreased electrical resistance (or increased conduction) at the points, indicating that the points are active and need treatment. Active Korean Hand Therapy points on the hands can be identified with these devices and electrical stimulation can be used to treat them. Dr. Yoo has developed an electrical stimulation device called the E-Beam to measure and stimulate Korean Hand Therapy points.

Another type of electrical stimulation device that does not use batteries or AC current is a piezo stimulator. The end of a pen-shaped device with crystals inside it is clicked to release an electric spark from the tip. The snapping sound can be loud and the mild electric shock can be a little uncomfortable, but it is a useful way to stimulate Korean Hand Therapy points.

Moxa

Moxibustion is the process of burning the dried herb moxa (Artemesia Vulgaris or mugwort) on the skin and it is often used in acupuncture treatment with or without needles. Small amounts of moxa are commonly burned on Korean Hand Therapy points in Korea and Japan, but this practice is much less popular in the Western world. Moxibustion is done as a preventative treatment for health promotion in Korean Hand Therapy, as well as to stimulate points to treat various problems, especially chronic conditions. Care must be taken to avoid burning the skin accidentally.

Needles

In Korea and Japan, small hand needles are the preferred method of stimulating Korean Hand Therapy points because they provide a strong stimulation and rapid results. Because the skin on the hand is thicker than other parts of the body, special needle inserters are required to get the needles into the skin.

Laser Therapy

Lasers are a concentrated form of light that is often use as an alternative to needles in acupuncture. Laser devices can be expensive and require the use of special goggles to protect the eyes. The power of a laser and the thickness of the skin in a particular part of the body determines how long each point should be treated, so special training is required to use them safely and effectively. Common laser pointers can be used to stimulate hand points but the treatment time would be long because they are weak lasers.

Color Light Therapy

I have met practitioners who treat Korean Hand Therapy points with various wavelengths produced by lights of different colors. This can be done alone or in combination with blunt pressure and press pellets. Some practitioners also use different colored lights on the hand at the points that correspond to the locations of Chakras on the body.

Crystals/Gemstones

Small stones can be taped to the hand at active correspondence points. This provides stimulation from blunt pressure as well as the benefit of special characteristics of different crystals and gems.

Homeopathic Tablets

I know a few homeopathy practitioners who tape homeopathic tablets to hands at active Korean Hand Therapy points. They report an added benefit of stimulating the point on the hand with the same homeopathic remedy that is taken by mouth.

Essential Oils

Advocates of essential oils have integrated their use with Correspondence Korean Hand Therapy. After locating and stimulating tender points on the hands, an appropriate essential oil is selected based on the particular problem that is being treated. A drop of the oil is placed on the hand point and is allowed to absorb into the skin.

Strategies for Treating Pain

Keep It Simple

It is easy to overthink things when you first learn Correspondence Korean Hand Therapy. The system really is as simple as searching for the precise points and stimulating them after you find them.

Following the same sequence of steps every time will reduce the chance of searching the wrong area of the hand and will increase the likelihood that you get the most effective results. It is a good idea to systemize the approach to looking for points and treating them.

For people with high pain tolerances, it is important to identify points that are more tender/sensitive/uncomfortable than others. You can probably endure much more discomfort than you feel when active points are located on the hands, but that is not the goal when searching for points. Nor is it important to give the points on the hands pain scores or compare the level of pain from one point to another. Consider it a simple yes or no question when you check each point - is it uncomfortable or not.

There is no added benefit to treating both hands. Use the right hand for problems on the right side of the body. Use the left hand for problems on the left side of the body. Only in unusual situations, like a missing limb, hands with severe damage or burns, lymphedema or other medical situations where pressure and probing is contraindicated, will you need to use the opposite hand.

Headaches

With most headaches, the problem is rarely limited to just where pain is located. The muscles of the head have multiple points of connection on the skull. Muscle tension in one area produces muscle tension in others, even if you are not aware of it. The muscles under the forehead are connected to the muscles on the back of the head which end at the occiput. After locating tender points in the area corresponding to the location of pain in your head, search the area above and below the first joint on the back of the middle finger, corresponding to the occiput. Treating only the areas that correspond to the headache pain will work, but the results will be better if you treat the tender points that are hiding around the occiput.

With a headache, there may be additional tender points in the area corresponding to the back of the neck, between the first and second joints on the back of the middle finger. Locating and stimulating additional tender points in this area will result in further reductions in headache pain.

For migraine headache pain, first search for the points that correspond to the location of the pain in the head. Afterward, locate the areas on the palm side of the middle finger that correspond to the eyes and bridge of the nose. Search for tender points in the areas on the finger above and below the eyes, corresponding to the frontal and max- illary sinuses. The ethmoid sinuses are directly under the bridge of the nose point. Migraine headaches are often trig- gered by subtle sinus problems and if the corresponding areas on the finger are tender, treating them will produce better headache relief.

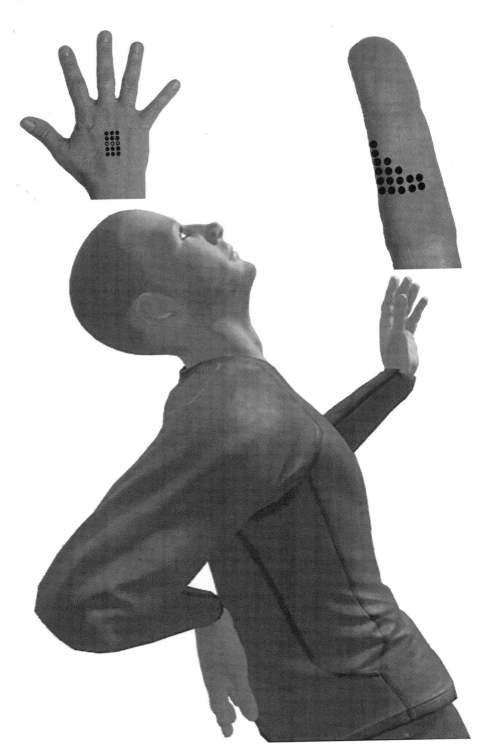

Neck and Back Pain

When treating pain located in the back of your neck, first search the corresponding area on the back of your middle finger, between the first and second joints. Even if the pain is only located on the back part of the neck, there will often be tender points in the area corresponding to the occiput because several neck muscles have their origins in this area. Searching for additional points above the first joint on the back of the middle finger and stimulating those you find will give you better pain relief of your neck pain.

Some muscles in the back of the neck wrap around the front side of the neck and attach to the collarbones. Search the palm side of the middle finger, between the first and second joints, for further reductions in neck pain.

Back pain close to the spine often seems limited to a specific area and the corresponding points on the back of the hand are easily located. However, there are often muscle spasms in the areas above and below where we feel pain in our backs. If you only stimulate the tender points in this area, the pain will decrease but you may notice that the pain "moves" afterwards to nearby areas. A better approach is to first locate the tender points on the back of the hand that correspond to where you feel the pain, then search the adjacent areas above, below and on either side of the primary location. This will result in a more dramatic reduction of pain and it will save you the trouble of having to repeat the process to "chase the pain" as you later become aware of pain at secondary locations.

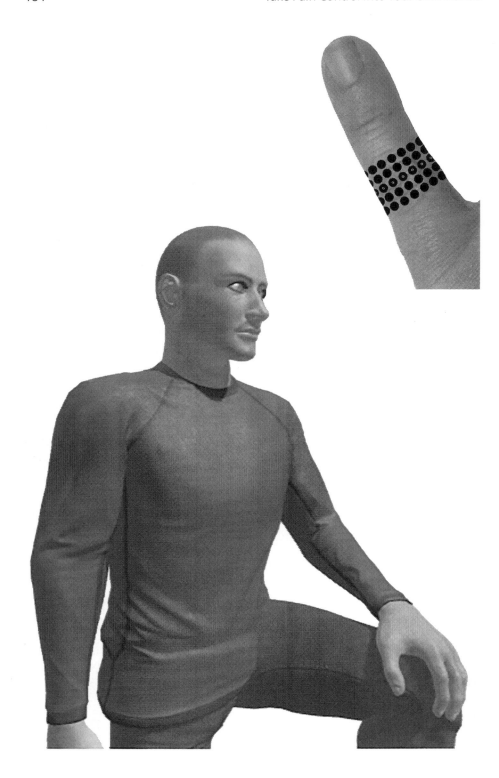

Joint Pains

In general, people are unable to identify the area of their joints where an injury has occurred. Pain that is felt in a specific location is often due to damage in a different area if x-rays and MRIs are done to evaluate it. Treating joint pains with Correspondence Korean Hand Therapy takes longer because a more comprehensive search is needed for maximum results.

Start with a search of the joint on the hand corresponding to where you feel the pain in the joint in your body. Even if your pain is significantly improved after stimulating the points, you are likely missing other tender points that directly correspond to the sites of injury inside the joint.

Next, locate the space between the bones of the corresponding finger joint, which represents the joint space in the joint in the body. This is where the cartilage of the joint is located and where degenerative changes frequently occur. Carefully search all the way around the finger in this area, marking any additional tender points you find.

Finally, do a comprehensive search above and below the joint line to make sure the entire surface area of the joint is checked for tender points. In order not to miss any areas, search in continuous rows all the way around the joint. It usually takes two or more rows above and two or more rows below the joint line to search the entire joint without missing any spots. It can be a bit tedious, but do not be tempted to skip searching the entire joint if you want the maximum relief from your joint pain.

Summary of Important Points

- The palm of the hand is the front of the body and the back of the hand is the back of the body.

- With your hands held facing outward, the right side of both hands is the right side of the body and left side of both hands is the left side of the body.

- Move your body to better localize the pain.

- Pointing to the painful location on the body will help identify the corresponding location on the hand.

- To avoid left-right confusion, hold your hands up with palms out first. After you locate the search area on the hand, bring the hand closer to you to search that area for specific points.

- Use the pinky, ring finger, and middle finger on the same side of the body in most cases.

- Avoid the nails. Do not press to locate or treat points on them.

- Locate and mark painful points.

- Check all the way around joints.

- Points that are red or purplish after pressure are usually active points that should be treated.

- Stimulate the points with three rounds of blunt pressure.

- Recheck the pain and range of motion in your body.

- Repeat the above steps if there is no improvement or if the pain has moved.

Draw Your Own Map

In my Correspondence Korean Hand Therapy workshops, I alway include time for drawing the corresponding body parts on blank drawings of the palm and back sides of the hand. The simple act of drawing it yourself helps embed the information into your brain and you will have a customized and complete map to refer to when you are done. The beauty of Correspondence Korean Hand Therapy is that the map of the body on the hands is logical and easy to memorize. The completed drawings are at the end of this chapter.

Please consider going through the exercise in this chapter to draw your own map. Creating a reference map with the landmarks in your own style will make it easier to understand when you look at it later. There is no right or wrong way to do it. You can even use colored pens or pencils and laminate the finished pages if you prefer. Before the step-by-step exercises, there are single-sided pages of the front and the back of the hand that you can photocopy or carefully cut out of this book. If you would rather draw on larger versions of the hands or would like a color copy of the completed drawings, you can download them at Take-PainControl.com .

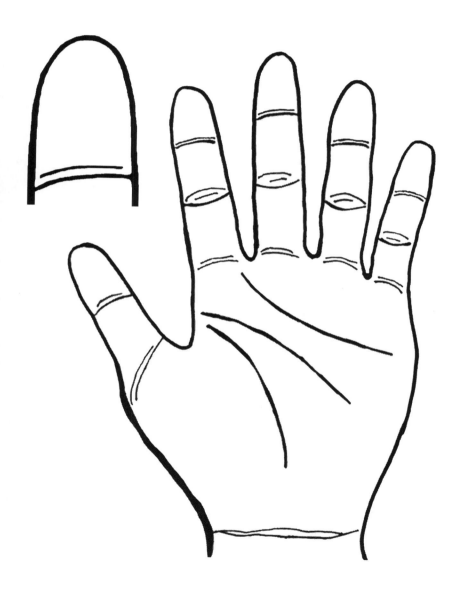

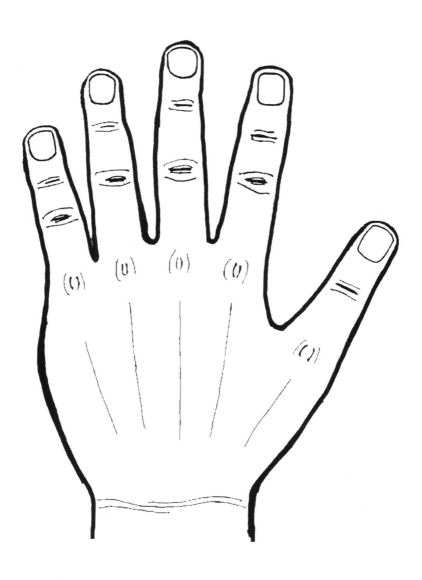

Front of the Body on the Palm of the Hand

We will begin with the palm side of the hand, representing the front of the body. The enlarged fingertip at the top left of the page will be used to draw the details of the tip of the middle finger, representing the face. We will draw the maps on the middle, ring and pinky fingers but you may choose to duplicate the landmarks from the ring finger onto the index finger and duplicate the landmarks from the pinky finger onto the thumb. If you get lost at any point, go back to the previous step or skip to the completed map at the end of this chapter to get yourself re-oriented.

Start with the blank drawing of the palm side of the hand. Label the drawing as "Left Hand" and remember the mirror image of this palm side hand map is on the palm side of the right hand.

The Palm Side of the Middle Finger

1.   Mark the tip of the middle finger as the Top of the Head.

2.   Mark the group of creases at the first joint as the Chin. This is also the Upper Neck.

3.   Draw an oval between the Top of the Head and Chin to represent the face that is between these landmarks.

4.   Mark the lowest part of the group of creases at the second joint as the Suprasternal Notch. This is also the Lower Neck.

5.   Mark the area where the middle finger meets the palm, as the Xiphoid Process. (Remember, this is not the third joint.)

6.   Follow the middle finger down to the bottom of the hand and mark the Perineum, where the muscles curve in above the wrist creases.

7.   Mark the halfway point between the Xiphoid Process and the Perineum, at approximately the center of the palm, as the Umbilicus or Bellybutton.

The Palm Side of the Tip of the Middle Finger

1.   Mark the tip of of the enlarged middle finger as the Top of the Head.

2.   Mark the first group of creases as the Chin.

3.   Find the halfway point between the Top of the Head and the Chin and mark it as the Bridge of the Nose. Draw a nose in this area with the nostrils below that point.

4.   Find the halfway point between the Top of the Head and the Bridge of the Nose and mark it as Between the Eyebrows. On either side of that point, draw the eyebrows and slightly below them, draw the left and right eyes.

5.   Find the halfway point between the Bridge of the Nose and the Chin and mark it as Between the Lips.

6.   Draw ears on both sides of the tip of the middle finger. The tops of the ears should be at the level of the Between the Eyebrows point. The bottoms of the ears should be between the Bridge of the Nose and the Between the Lips levels.

The Palm Side of the Ring Finger

1.   Mark the group of creases at the first joint as the Wrist joint.

2.   Draw a little hand between the tip of the ring finger and the first group of creases. Your drawing should show the thumb of the little hand is on the medial side of the finger, closest to the middle finger.

3.   Mark the lowest part of the group of creases at the second joint as the Elbow joint.

4.   Mark the elbow protrusion on the lateral edge of the ring finger (closest to the pinky finger), at the level of the Elbow joint. Use a half circle to indicate that only half of the elbow protrusion is on the palm side of the hand.

5.   Mark the third joint with a large circle as the Shoulder joint. Remember that the Shoulder joint includes almost the entire area from where the ring finger meets the palm to the large crease running across the palm under the ring finger.

The Palm Side of the Pinky Finger

1.   Mark the group of creases at the first joint as the Ankle joint.

2.   Draw a little foot between the tip of the pinky finger and the first group of creases. Your drawing should show the big toe of the little foot is on the medial side of the finger, closest to the ring finger.

3.   Mark the lowest part of the group of creases at the second joint as the Knee joint.

4.   Mark the kneecap on the medial edge of the pinky finger (closest to the ring finger), at the level of the Knee joint. Use a half circle to indicate that only half of the kneecap is on the palm side of the hand.

5.   Mark the third joint with a large circle as the Hip joint. Remember that the Hip joint includes almost the entire area from where the pinky finger meets the palm to the large crease running across the palm under the pinky finger.

Back of the Body on the Back of the Hand

Now move on to the back side of the hand, representing the back of the body. We will draw the maps on the middle, ring and pinky fingers but you may choose to duplicate the landmarks from the ring finger onto the index finger and duplicate the landmarks from the pinky finger onto the thumb. If you get lost at any point, go back to the previous step or skip to the completed map at the end of this chapter to get yourself re-oriented.

Use the blank drawing of the back side of the hand. Label the drawing as "Left Hand" and remember the mirror image of this back side hand map is on the back of the right hand.

The Back of the Middle Finger

1.   Mark the tip of the middle finger as the Top of the Head.

2.   Mark the center of the group of creases at the first joint as C1-C2 or Occiput. This is also the Upper Neck.

3.   Mark the center of the group of creases at the second joint as C7-T1. This is also the Lower Neck.

4.   Mark the center of the third joint (the knuckle) as T7-T8. This is also the Mid Back.

5.   Between the second and third joints, find the point- about one quarter of the way down. Draw two triangles pointing down on either side of the midline of the finger with a space left between them to represent the scapulas or shoulder blades.

6.   Follow the middle finger down to the bottom of the hand and mark the Coccyx or Tailbone at the tip of the tri- angle-shaped indentation above the wrist creases.

7.   Mark the halfway point between T7-T8 and the Coc- cyx, at approximately the center of the back of the hand, as L2-L3. This is also the Low Back.

8.   Draw lines or little arrows along both sides of the middle finger, about three quarters of the way down the back of the hand. Draw lines to connect these two points and the Coccyx to mark the triangle-shaped Sacrum.

The Back of the Ring Finger

1.   Mark the center of the group of creases at the first joint as the Wrist joint.

2.   Draw a little hand between the tip of the ring finger and the first group of creases. Your drawing should show the thumb of the little hand is on the medial side of the finger, closest to the middle finger.

3.   Mark the center of the group of creases at the second joint as the Elbow joint.

4.   Mark the elbow protrusion on the lateral edge of the ring finger (closest to the pinky finger), at the level of the Elbow joint. Use a half circle to indicate that only half of the elbow protrusion is on the back side of the hand.

5.   Mark the third joint (the knuckle) with a large circle as the Shoulder joint.

The Back of the Pinky Finger

1.   Mark the center of the group of creases at the first joint as the Ankle joint.

2.   Draw a little foot between the tip of the pinky finger and the first group of creases. Your drawing should show the big toe of the little foot is on the medial side of the finger, closest to the ring finger.

3.   Mark the center of the group of creases at the second joint as the Knee joint.

4.   Mark the kneecap on the medial edge of the pinky finger (closest to the ring finger), at the level of the Knee joint. Use a half circle to indicate that only half of the actual knee protrusion is on the back side of the body and hand.

5.   Mark the third joint (the knuckle) with a large circle as the Hip joint.

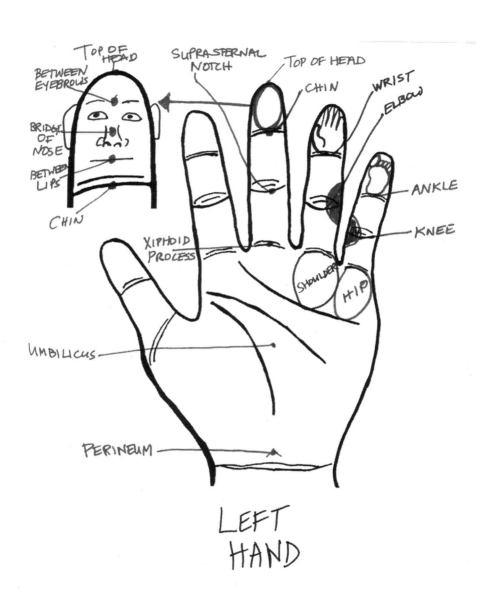

LEFT
HAND

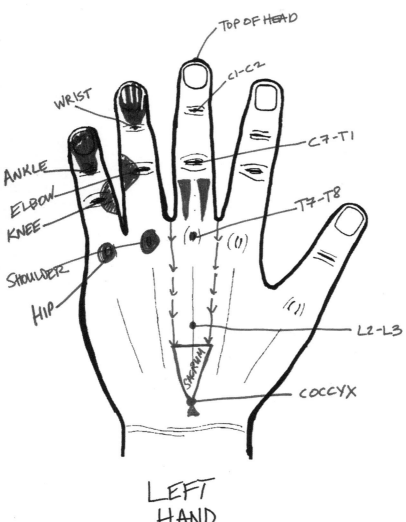

TOP OF HEAD

C1-C2

WRIST

C7-T1

ANKLE

ELBOW

KNEE

T7-T8

SHOULDER

HIP

SACRUM

L2-L3

COCCYX

LEFT
HAND

"The two enemies of human happiness are
pain and boredom."

- Arthur Schopenhauer

Practice What You Have Learned

When you put what you have learned to use, it sticks inside your head better. With Correspondence Korean Hand Therapy, it is important to practice identifying key locations on the hands. To test your knowledge, this chapter has photographs of different areas of the hand for you to identify with the answer provided on the back of each page.

Carefully look at each photograph, focusing on the location on the hand indicated by the tip of the probe and ask yourself the following questions:

- Is this the palm side or back side of the hand?

- Is this area located on the middle finger (or directly below it), the ring finger, or the pinky finger?

- What landmarks are located directly above and below this one?

- What part of the body does this area represent?

At the end of the chapter is also a list of the steps needed to use this system. Finally, I have committed to do monthly live webinars for at least one year after this book is published. Anyone can submit questions in advance and the webinars will be archived if you cannot attend live. Upcoming webinar dates will be posted on TakePainControl.com .

Name the Corresponding Body Area

On the next pages are photographs pointing out areas on the front and back of the hand. Write down the name of the corresponding body area and flip the page over to check the answer. The description of the location is also provided.

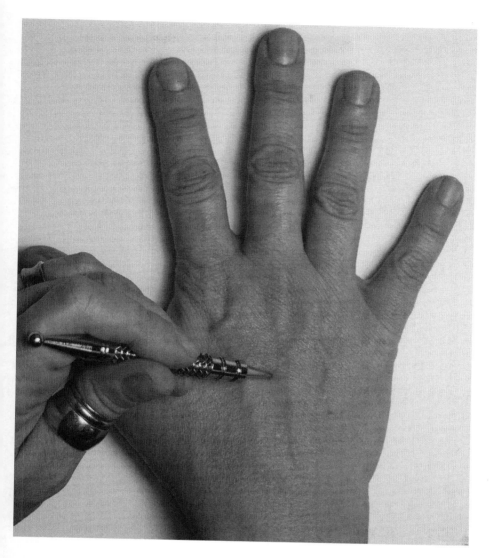

1. Corresponding Body Area:_____

_____

_____

1. Corresponding Body Area:

L2-L3 (also Low Back).

(Back side of hand, halfway between T7-T8 and Coccyx)

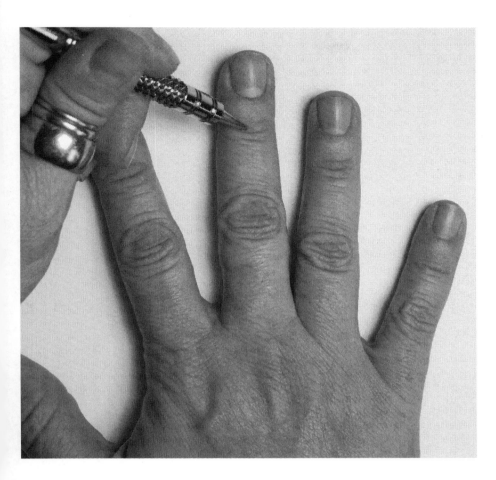

2. Corresponding Body Area:_____

_____

_____

2. Corresponding Body Area:

C1-C2 or Occiput (also back of Upper Neck).

(Back side of hand, middle finger, first joint)

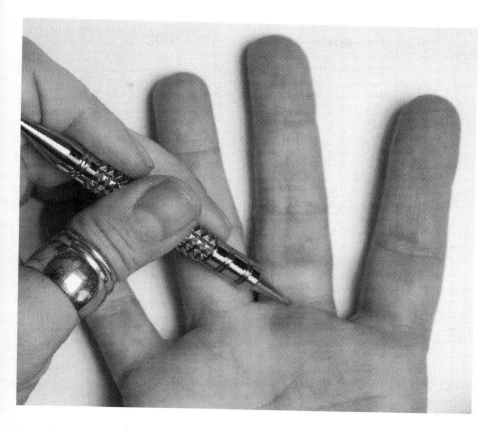

3. Corresponding Body Area:_____

_____

_____

3. Corresponding Body Area:

Xiphoid Process (where the ribs meet at the lower center of the chest).

(Palm side of hand, where the middle finger meets the palm)

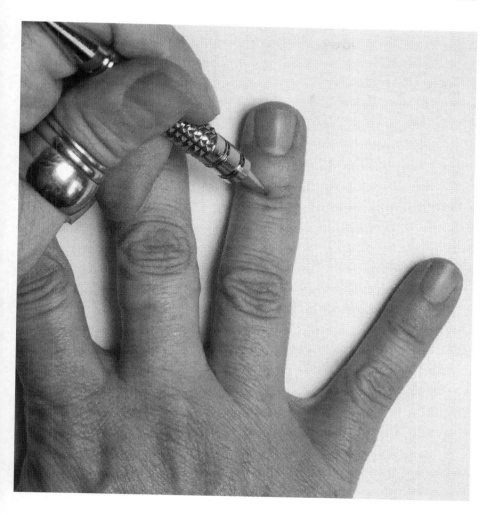

4. Corresponding Body Area:_____

_____

_____

4. Corresponding Body Area:

Back side of the Wrist joint

(Back side of hand, ring finger, first joint)

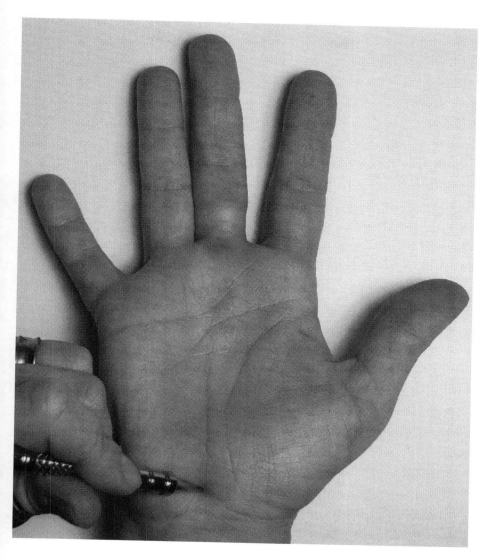

5. Corresponding Body Area:_____
_____
_____

5. Corresponding Body Area:

Perineum (area between genitals and anus).

(Palm side of hand, down the center of the middle finger, just above the wrist creases, where the muscles in the lower palm curve in)

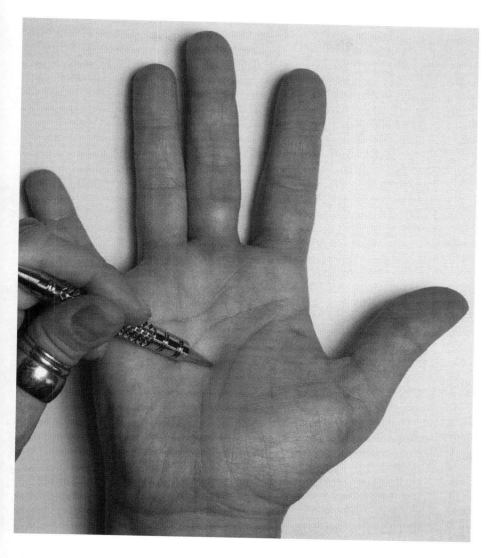

6. Corresponding Body Area:_____

_____

_____

6. Corresponding Body Area:

Umbilicus or Bellybutton.

(Palm side of hand, halfway between the Xiphoid Process and Perineum)

7. Corresponding Body Area:_____

_____

_____

7. Corresponding Body Area:

Back side of the Knee joint.

(Back side of hand, pinky finger, second joint)

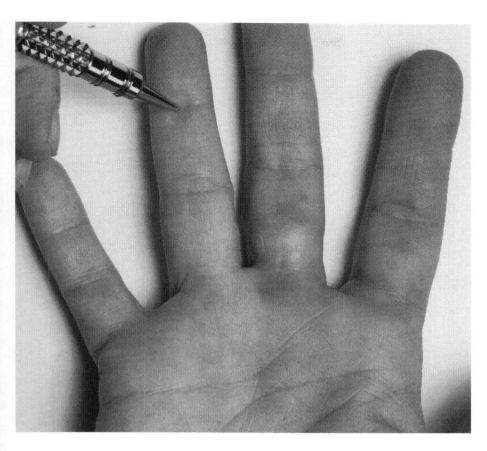

8. Corresponding Body Area:_____

_____

_____

8. Corresponding Body Area:

Front side of the Wrist joint.

(Palm side of hand, ring finger, first joint)

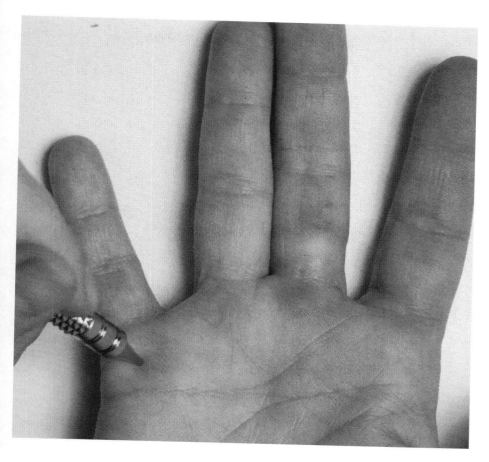

9. Corresponding Body Area:_____

_____

_____

9. Corresponding Body Area:

Front side of the Hip joint.

(Palm side of hand, pinky finger, third joint)

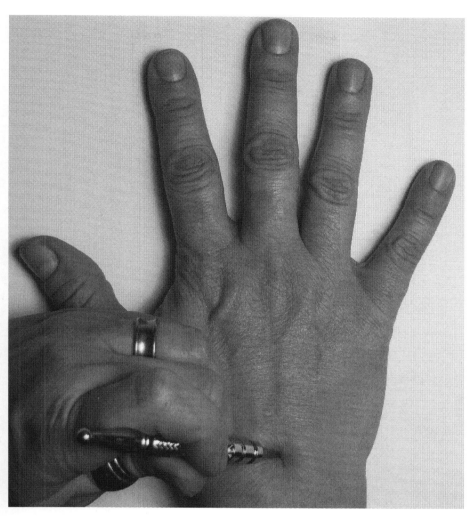

10. Corresponding Body Area:_____

_____

_____

10. Corresponding Body Area:

Coccyx or Tailbone.

(Back side of hand, down the center of the middle finger, just above the wrist creases, at the top part of the triangle-shaped indentation)

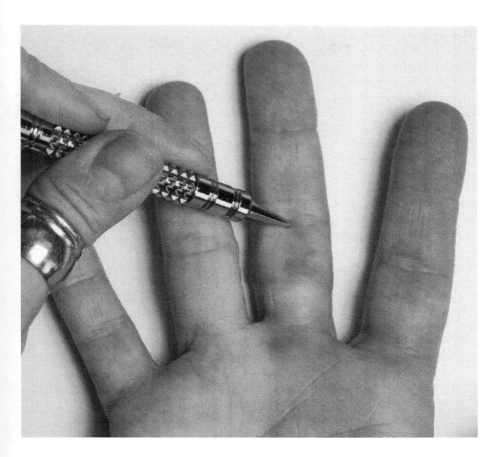

11. Corresponding Body Area:_____

_____

_____

11. Corresponding Body Area:

Suprasternal Notch (also front of Lower Neck).

(Palm side of hand, middle finger, second joint)

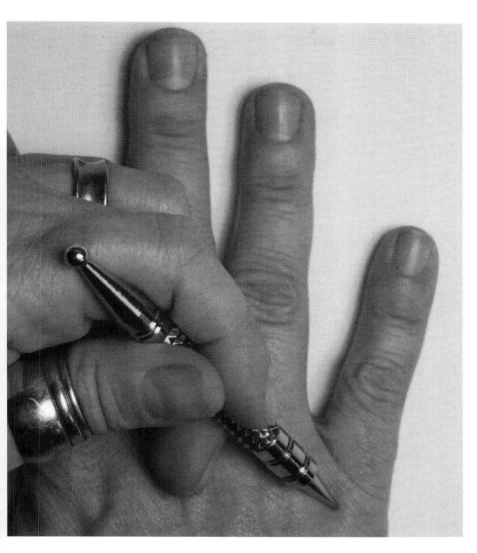

12. Corresponding Body Area:_____
_____
_____

12. Corresponding Body Area:

Back of the Hip joint.

(Back side of hand, pinky finger, third joint)

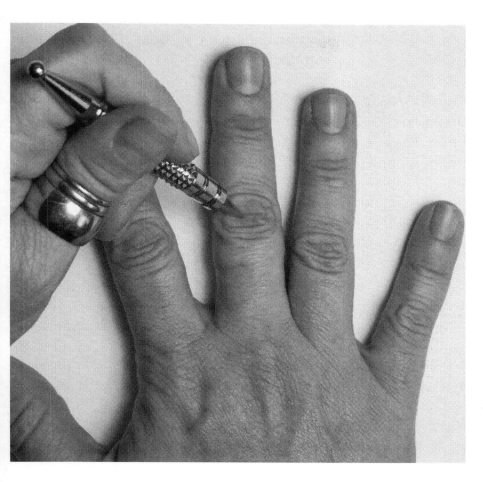

13. Corresponding Body Area:_____

_____

_____

13. Corresponding Body Area:

C7-T1 (also back of Lower Neck).

(Back side of hand, middle finger, second joint)

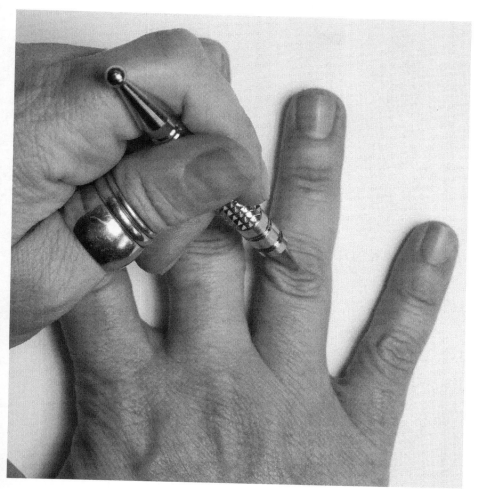

14. Corresponding Body Area:_____

_____

_____

14. Corresponding Body Area:

Back of the Elbow joint.

(Back side of hand, ring finger, second joint)

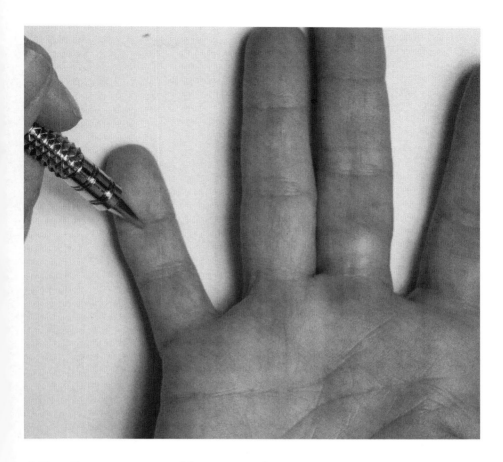

15. Corresponding Body Area:_____

_____

_____

15. Corresponding Body Area:

Front of the Ankle joint.

(Palm side of hand, pinky finger, first joint)

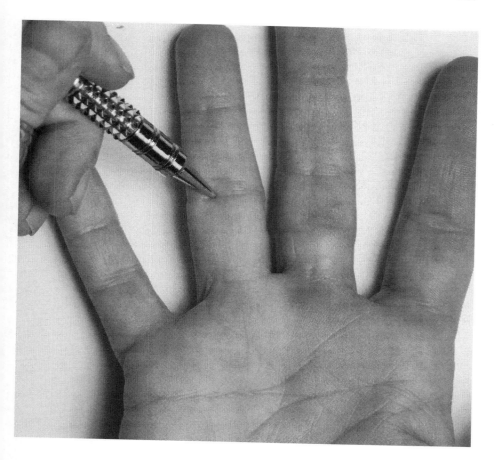

16. Corresponding Body Area:_____

16. Corresponding Body Area:

Front of the Elbow joint

(Palm side of hand, ring finger, second joint)

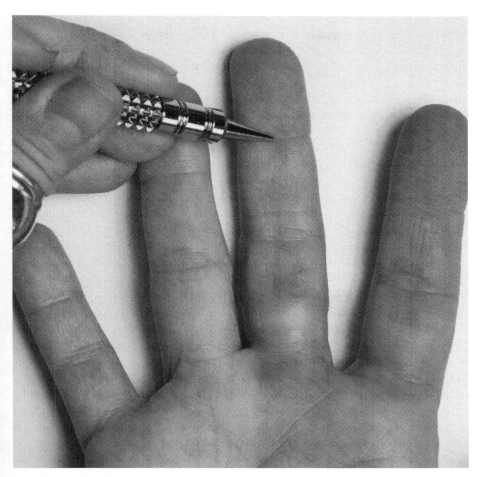

17. Corresponding Body Area:_____

_____

_____

17. Corresponding Body Area:

Chin.

(Palm side of hand, middle finger, first joint)

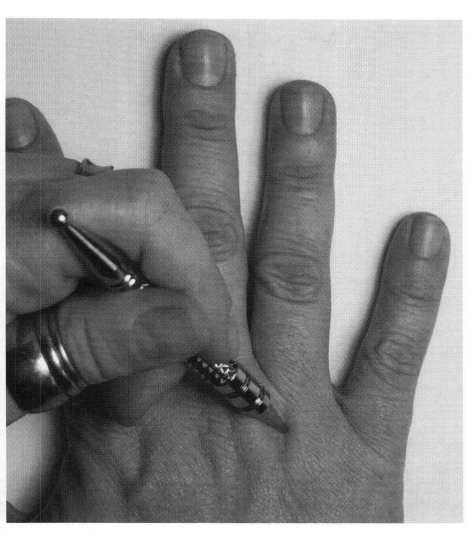

18. Corresponding Body Area:_____

_____

_____

18. Corresponding Body Area:

Back of the Shoulder joint.

(Back side of hand, ring finger, third joint)

Practice What You Have Learned

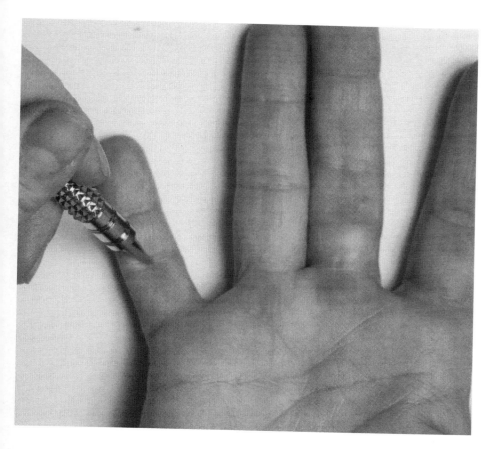

19. Corresponding Body Area:_____

_____

_____

19. Corresponding Body Area:

Front of the Knee joint.

(Palm side of hand, pinky finger, second joint)

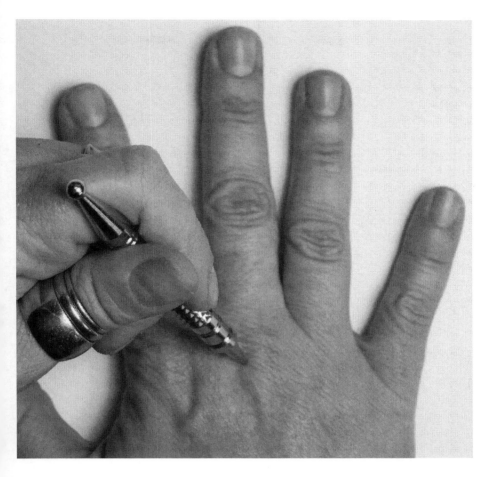

20. Corresponding Body Area:_____

_____

_____

20. Corresponding Body Area:

T7-T8 (also Mid Back).

(Back side of hand, middle finger, third joint)

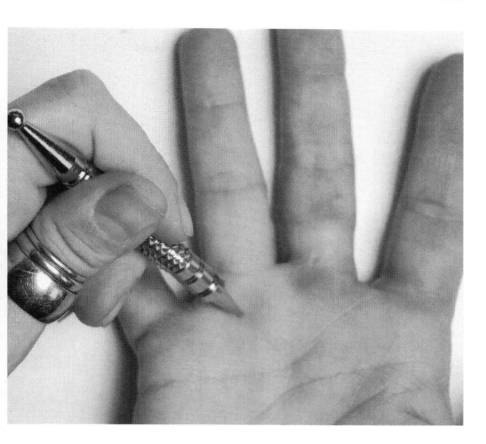

21. Corresponding Body Area:_____

_____

_____

21. Corresponding Body Area:

Front of the Shoulder joint.

(Palm side of hand, ring finger, third joint)

22. Corresponding Body Area:_____

_____

_____

22. Corresponding Body Area:

Back of the Ankle joint.

(Back side of hand, pinky finger, first joint)

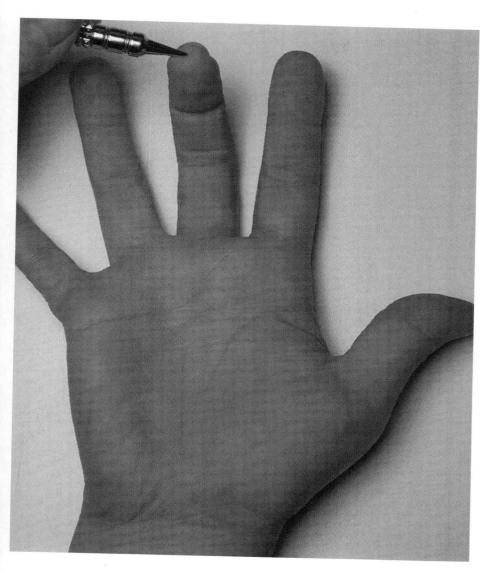

23. Corresponding Body Area:_____

_____

_____

23. Corresponding Body Area:

Top of the Head.

(Palm side of hand, middle finger, a few millimeters away from the underside of the nail)

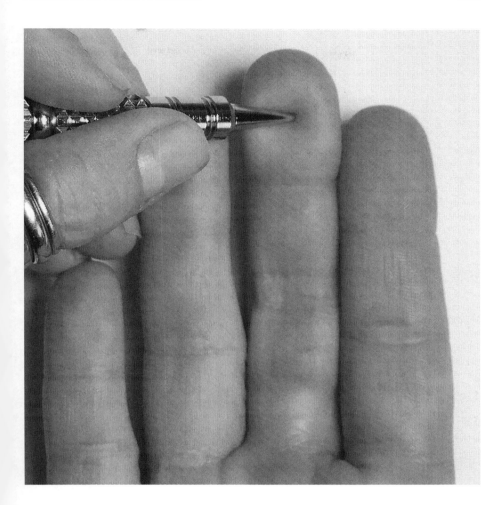

24. Corresponding Body Area:_____

_____

_____

24. Corresponding Body Area:

Nose.

(Palm side of hand, middle finger, halfway between the underside of the nail and the first joint)

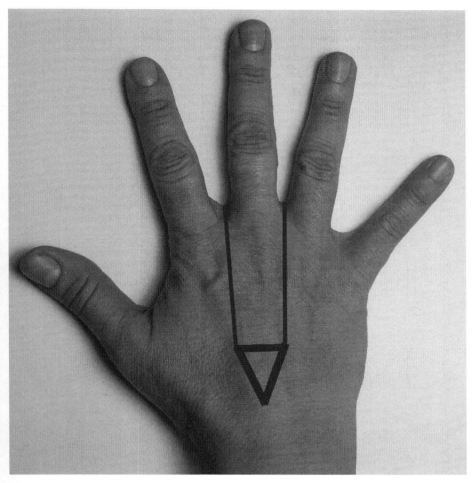

25. Corresponding Body Area:_____

_____

_____

25. Corresponding Body Area:

Sacrum.

(Back side of hand, in the triangle formed by going down both sides of the middle finger until you can go no further and the coccyx)

List of Steps to Follow

1. Point, with one finger, to where the pain is located in your body.

2. Is the pain on the right side, left side, or center of the body?

   So will you use the right hand or left hand?

3. Is the pain on the front or back of the body?

   So will you use the front or back side of the hand?

4. Where are the landmarks on the hand that are closest to the location of pain on the body?

5. Identify the search area.

6. Locate and mark the painful points.

7. Do three rounds of stimulating the points.

8. Recheck pain and your range of motion.

9. Repeat the above steps if no improvement or if the pain has moved.

"The aim of the wise is not to secure pleasure,
but to avoid pain."

- Aristotle

Case Studies

I am regularly asked about my experiences with Correspondence Korean Hand Therapy to treat pain in other people. Because of my continued curiosity and amazement with the efficacy of Korean Hand Therapy, I frequently treat the doctors and nurses I work with. I became curious to see if they would get some relief when they mentioned they were in pain during casual conversations at the hospital. Sometimes I am approached by co-workers of nurses and doctors I treated, after they heard stories about how their colleague's pain improved when I poked on their hands. I have also treated several of my son's teachers and some parents of his classmates after they told me they were in pain.

At first, I wanted to see if Correspondence Korean Hand Therapy really worked as well as I thought it did. Now I use it because I know it works. I still get excited about seeing the look on people's faces when their pain level promptly and unexpectedly drops in just a few minutes. I also use Correspondence Korean Hand Therapy to treat my own pain.

I hope you find these case studies interesting and that they inspire you to treat yourself with Korean Hand Therapy if you have similar problems. To encourage you to think about out what part of the hands to use for different pain problems, I have added a diagram of the treatment areas with each story. The case studies are all real, with minor details changed for privacy reasons.

Chin ➞

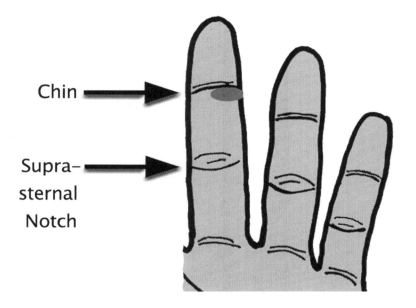

Supra–
sternal
Notch ➞

Sore Throat

I had several bouts of strep throat as a child and remember countless visits to the doctor for confirmatory testing and a course of antibiotics. Unfortunately, I must still be extremely susceptible to this infection and had a few episodes recently when my son and his classmates were sick. Luckily, I now have a better way to help manage the sore throat symptoms and I use it even before I make an appointment with my doctor.

With strep throat, I get an annoying pain in one side of my throat. It feels as if someone is standing next to me all the time, with their finger firmly pressed into the side of my neck. The pain is constant and I dread swallowing because it makes the pain unbearable. Even after starting antibiotics, it takes a day or two for the pain to subside.

The pain is usually located on one side of the front of my upper neck, under the angle of the lower jaw. I can easily find corresponding tender points on the palm side of my middle finger, below the level of the first joint. Pressing on this area with my fingernail or the tip of a ballpoint pen produces an instantaneous reduction in the pain with swallowing. If I place one or two press pellets on the most tender points and securely tape them to my finger, the pain improves so much that I almost forget that I have a throat infection.

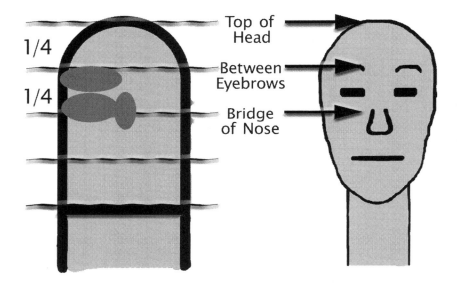

Top of
Head

1/4

Between
Eyebrows

1/4

Bridge
of Nose

Sinus Headache

I overheard one of the nurse practitioners complaining about a headache above and below her eyes from her sinus infection. Her nose was red and congested and she could barely keep her eyes open because of the pain. I offered to help her and she readily agreed. As I poked at the palm side of her middle fingertip, I guessed that her headache was more on the right side than the left because I found more tender points on the right side of her finger.

While I was focused on her finger, she suddenly asked me to look at her face. I did not understand why she would ask me to look at her face, so I kept my eyes fixed on her finger and continued my search for points. When she repeated her request, I looked up. Her nose was noticeably less red and she said she could feel the congestion in her nose dry up as I was poking on her finger. I was genuinely surprised and told her I did not know Korean Hand Therapy could do that. I asked about her headache and she said it was better too.

I saw her several hours later and she told me that when her symptoms worsened after the initial treatment, she used the tip of a pen to stimulate the points I had marked on her fingertip and the symptoms quickly disappeared again.

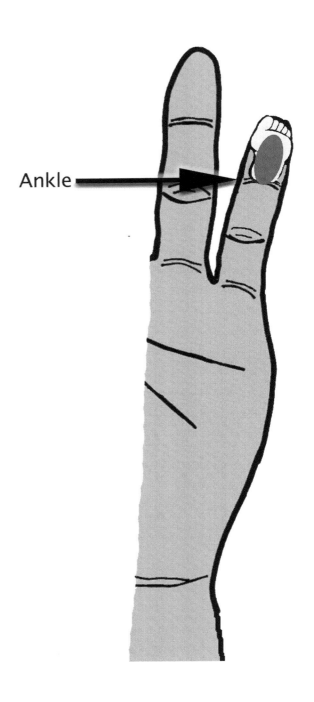

Ankle

Plantar Fasciitis

After watching me treating a nurse with back pain, another nurse asked if the technique I was using would work for plantar fasciitis too. I told her I had never tried it for that problem, but I had no reason to think it would not work. She told me she had plantar fasciitis in both feet and, as an intensive care nurse, she had few breaks during her shifts at work. When the pain became severe, sitting and resting helped a little but she had to continue working in pain.

The soles of the feet are represented on the palm side of the left and right pinky fingers. There was not a single spot on either fingertip that was not tender to pressure with my probe. Rather than cover her fingertips with dots as I identified each point, I suggested she apply pressure to all areas on her pinky fingertips with a pen. She immediately had relief in the pain in her feet and I advised her to repeat the stimulation to the pinky fingertips whenever the pain flared again.

Several months later, I saw this nurse again at the hospital. She told me she had been telling everyone that I cured her plantar fasciitis. Embarrassed, I told her that this was not true and it would make the doctors and nurses we worked with think we were both crazy. She said she sometimes had pain in her feet, but it happened much less often than before. Whenever the pain returned, she pressed her thumbnails firmly into her pinky fingertips in several places to find the tender spots, with enough pressure to cause a little pain. When she walked again, she noticed the pain in her feet was improved and she could get back to work without thinking about her feet.

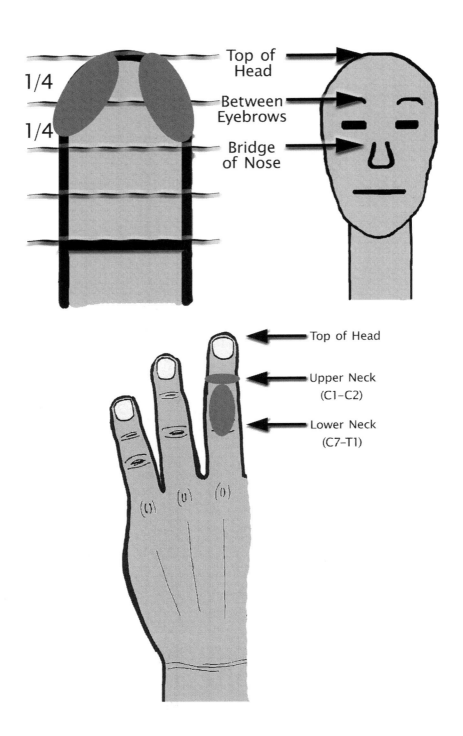

Frequent Headaches

A nurse I previously treated ran up to me and told me I needed to treat one of her colleagues right away for a severe headache. The other nurse was a former paratrooper with had chronic headaches from neck and back injuries. His job was to monitor the computer screens tracking the patients' heart rhythms, which gave him a headache by the end of each workday. That day's headache was especially bad. He said he tried several medications with no results and has now accepted that he will be in pain for the rest of his life.

When I approached him, he looked uncomfortable with a deep furrow in his brow and told me he doubted anything I tried would work. When I asked where his pain was located, he pointed to both sides of his head at the temples and said the pain is always in the same place. I found tender points on the front and sides of his middle fingertip. I then turned over his middle finger and found many more tender points corresponding to the occiput and neck. I activated all the points and showed him how to do the same with the tip of a ballpoint pen.

I asked him again how his headache felt. He stared at his finger that was dotted with marks and said nothing for a long. "I'm confused," he said. "My headache is almost gone, but that's not possible. All you did was poke on my finger. That's crazy." I told him to stimulate the points again when the headache returns and he should get the same results. Several months later, I saw him again. This time he was smiling. He said he poked on his fingers whenever he felt a headache start and he did not have any severe headaches since I last saw him.

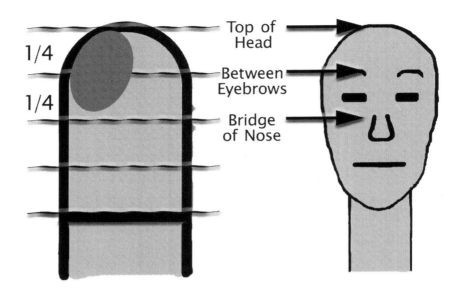

1/4

1/4

Top of Head

Between Eyebrows

Bridge of Nose

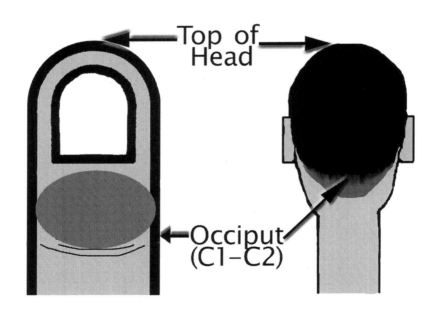

Top of Head

Occiput (C1–C2)

Frequent Migraine Headaches

I was asked to teach my workshop to the first year medical students. I thought Correspondence Korean Hand Therapy would be a great technique they could use right away on themselves and their families. After class, I was approached by one of the medical students who told me he gets frequent migraine headaches and asked if I thought Korean Hand Therapy would help him. He said he thought the workshop was interesting but he was still skeptical about it, even after seeing results in his classmates. He told me he had a right frontal headache at that time, so I offered to find the corresponding tender points on his hand.

I found several tender points on the palm side of his middle fingertip, in the areas corresponding to the right forehead and eye as well as a few points on the back side of the middle finger above the first joint. I marked and stimulated them, then asked the student how his head felt afterward. He looked a little confused and said, "It might be the placebo effect, but my headache just went away." He admitted that his headaches never disappear like that and they did not go away completely, even after taking medication for it.

He asked how poking on his finger could take away his headache and wondered if the mild discomfort I had caused on his fingertip was just a distraction technique, making him ignore the headache while focusing on a different pain. I asked him if he thought his headache would have gone away if I had stomped on his foot or kicked him in the shin, and he admitted that he did not think so. I told him to take a picture of his finger so he could easily find the points to stimulate them again when he had another migraine headache. I told him he would have plenty of opportunities to prove to himself that it wasn't the placebo effect making his headache go away when he tried it again.

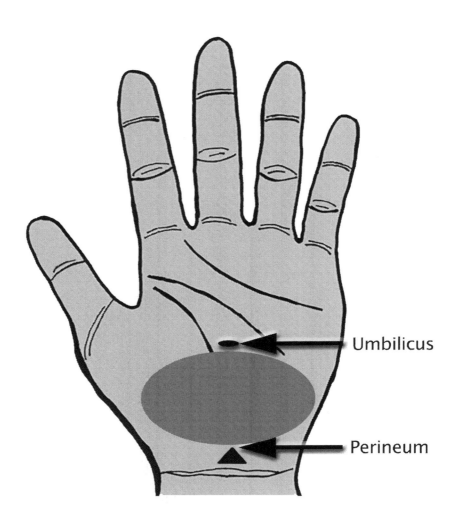

Menstrual Cramps

A doctor at the hospital called me over and whispered in my ear, "I have horrible period cramps and just took some ibuprofen but I'm in so much pain that I can't get my work done." The doctors and nurses often greeted me with "Hi, my back hurts!" instead of "Hi, how are you?" but I had never been asked about treating menstrual cramps. She told me that the pains were so debilitating that she sometimes had to spend a day in bed each month. I offered to try using Correspondence Korean Hand Therapy to help her, telling her I did not know what would happen but it would be an interesting experiment.

I checked the area on the palm side of her hand, between the umbilicus and perineum corresponding locations. She had many tender points in the center of this area with some on the right side but none of the left. I asked her if her cramps were mostly on the right side and she said yes.

After stimulating the points, I asked her how the pain was compared with before the treatment. She said the cramps were almost gone and she was sure the medication had not kicked in yet because it always took at least thirty minutes to work. I told her to press on the points again when the pain returns. Later, a nurse told me she heard about how I had helped the doctor with menstrual cramps. She wanted to know where those points on the hand are located because she also suffered with bad cramps each month.

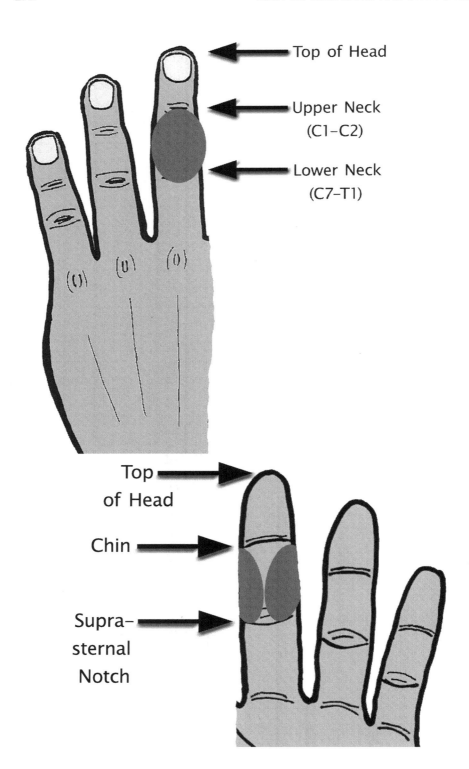

Top of Head

Upper Neck
(C1–C2)

Lower Neck
(C7–T1)

Top
of Head

Chin

Supra-
sternal
Notch

Migraines and Neck Pain After Car Accident

A nurse overheard my conversation with another nurse I had previously treated and asked me if I could help her too. She often had severe migraine headaches and chronic neck pains after a serious car accident several years earlier. She told me she detested taking pain medication and waited until the headache pain became intolerable before she would take any medication.

I found several tender points on the back of her middle finger, above the first joint and between the first and second joints, corresponding to the occiput and the back of the neck. I also found a few points on the palm side of the middle finger, between the first and second joints, corresponding to the muscles that wrap around to the front of the neck. Right away, she noticed reduced pain and reported loosening of the muscles in her neck. I told her to stimulate the points again when her neck pain gets worse or as soon as a headache starts.

A few months later, I saw her again at the hospital. I was surprised to hear that she had not had a severe migraine in months. She told me whenever her neck pain becomes bothersome or when she feels a headache start, she takes a ballpoint pen and presses on the corresponding points for rapid relief. Because she does a lot of driving to and from work, she sometimes does this in her car with her hand perched on the steering wheel while stopped at an intersection. Even though she sometimes gets strange looks from other drivers, she did not care because she the pain relief is immediate.

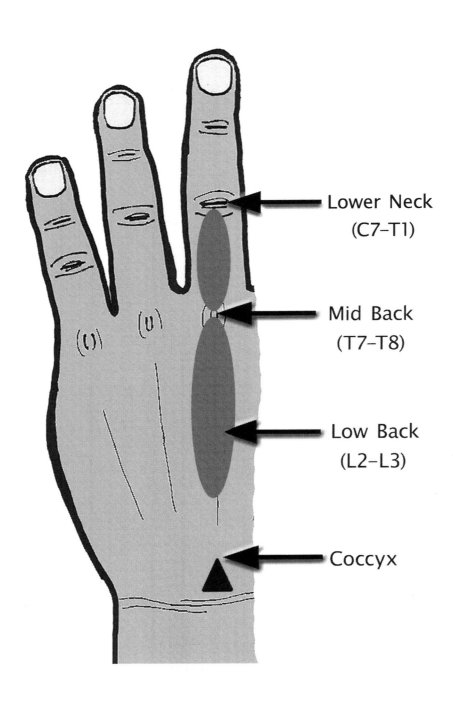

Lower Neck
(C7–T1)

Mid Back
(T7–T8)

Low Back
(L2–L3)

Coccyx

Chronic Back Pain

A pharmacist mentioned her low back pain while we were discussing a patient in the hospital. She had heard about my use of Korean Hand Therapy from one of the nurses and she was intrigued by the idea that pain could be reduced by poking on one's hands. She told me she had chronic low back pain that became worse after moving into a new home and sleeping on an air mattress every night while waiting to buy a new bed. Unable to get a restful night of sleep, she was exhausted at work each day and needed over-the-counter medications for the pain. When I asked her where the pain was located, she pointed to her low back. I found several tender points on the back of her hand, below the middle finger, in the area corresponding to her low back. After marking and stimulating the points, I asked her to recheck the pain by standing up and walking around.

She reported that her low back was better but now her middle and upper back were sore. I explained that the new pain had alway been there but was overshadowed by the more severe low back pain. I found more tender points along the back of her middle finger. When she rechecked her pain, she was surprised how much better it was. I told her to take a picture of the marked points on her hand so she could find them again and treat herself when the pain returned.

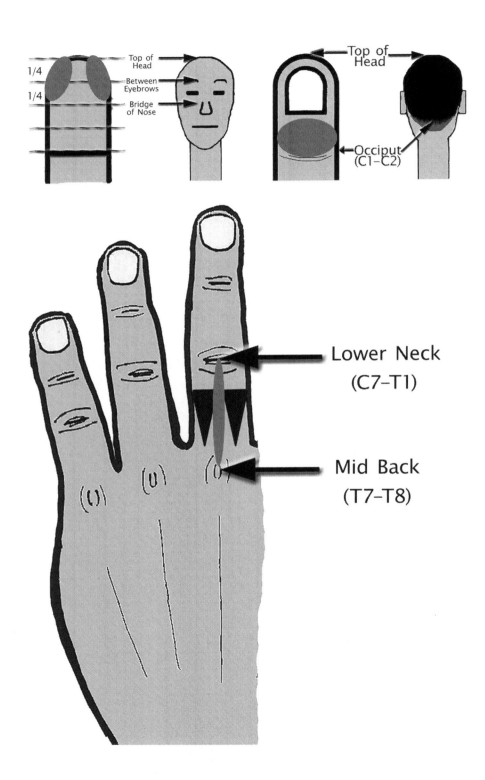

Headache and Chronic Upper Back Pain

A nurse I treated in the past asked me to help one of her colleagues who was having a bad headache that day. The other nurse told me that her headache was so bad that she was considering going home. She pointed to her temples and said it felt like her head was being squeezed. I found tender points on the edges and palm side of her midde fingertip, as well as the back side of the middle fingertip. She reported that her headache was better right away.

As I was about to leave, she told me that her more severe pain problem was debilitating pains in her middle back, between the shoulder blades. The pain was so bad that she often could not sleep. On the back of her middle finger, I found several tender points in the area corresponding to the area between the scapulas and marked them for her. After I activated the points with my probe, she reported that the muscles in that area felt more loose and the pain had decreased. I advised her to stimulate the tender points again whenever her pain got worse.

As soon as she saw me again a few months later, she ran up to me, gave me a big hug, and told me I that I changed her life. At first I thought she was joking, but tears welled up in her eyes as she spoke. She frequently massages the points on her finger corresponding to the area between her shoulder blades and firmly pokes them when the pain flares. Her sleep had improved and she woke up pain-free each morning. She told me that she stopped taking a muscle relaxant she was using for severe muscle tension. She told me that she stopped it on her own because she no longer needed it and she disliked how it made her groggy the next day.

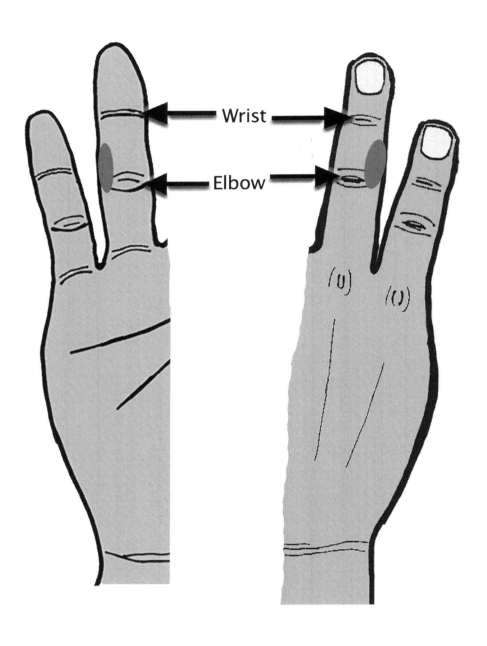

Tennis Elbow/Mouse Elbow

I noticed one of the nurses was holding her right arm in a strange position while we were discussing a patient. She told me she was recently diagnosed with tennis elbow, also known as lateral epicondylitis, from spending long periods typing on the computer at work. Her doctor told her the problem is so common in people who use computers that it is now also nicknamed "mouse elbow." She was advised to rest her arm, but that was not possible as the nurses have to use computers all day to access the patients' electronic medical records.

I offered to treat her with Correspondence Korean Hand Therapy and she happily agreed. She showed me where she felt the pain, pointing right below her lateral right elbow and said it sometimes radiated further down towards her hand.

I found tender points on the back side of her right ring finger, just above the second joint, on the side closest to the pinky finger. There were also a few points on the palm side of the ring finger in the same area. After stimulating the points, she extended her arm and rotated her wrist several times. She noticed the pain was better but now felt some discomfort a little further down her arm. I did a second search and found only one more tender point in the new area. After stimulating all the points again, she reported that the pain was much improved. I advised her to take a picture of the points I had marked on her finger so she could stimulate them when the pain returned. I also gave her some press pellets to apply to the points overnight.

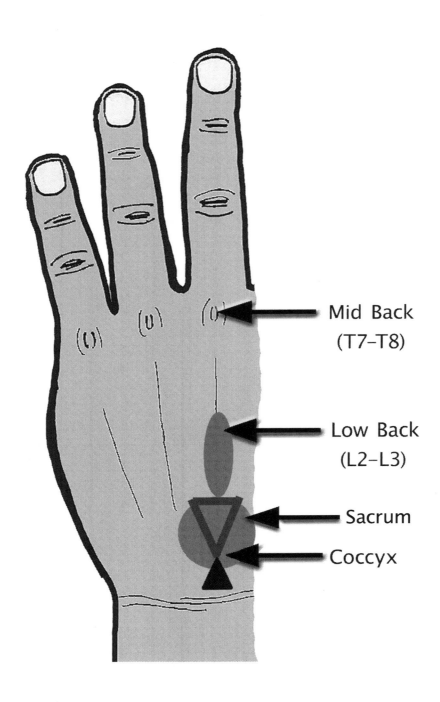

Mid Back
(T7–T8)

Low Back
(L2–L3)

Sacrum

Coccyx

Low Back Pain

A nurse stopped me in the hallway. He had seen me treat other nurses and wondered if I could help him. He often had pain in the middle of the lumbar area of his back that worsened when he stood up from a chair or after standing for long periods of time. Because pain medications upset his stomach, he did not like to take them at work. Sometimes the pain was so bad when he got home from work that he had to take medication because the pain kept him from falling asleep.

Because his pain was in the center of his body, either hand could be used for treatment. He was right-handed and I chose his left hand so it would be easier for him to treat himself with his dominant hand. Using the back of his hand, I looked at the knuckle of his middle finger (corresponding to the T7-T8 area) and the area corresponding to the coccyx by the wrist. I searched the area halfway between them, representing the L2-L3 area.

There were only a few tender points corresponding to where he had pain and I dotted them with a marker. I stimulated the points and he noticed the pain was much better right away. But now he reported pain in a new place - further down his back, on the upper part of his sacrum. I searched further down on the back of his hand toward the area representing the coccyx, where I found and stimulated several more tender points. Afterwards, he stood up, walked around, and repeatedly sat down and got up from his chair. He then declared that his back pain was gone. I advised him to stimulate those points again with the tip of his pen when the pain returned.

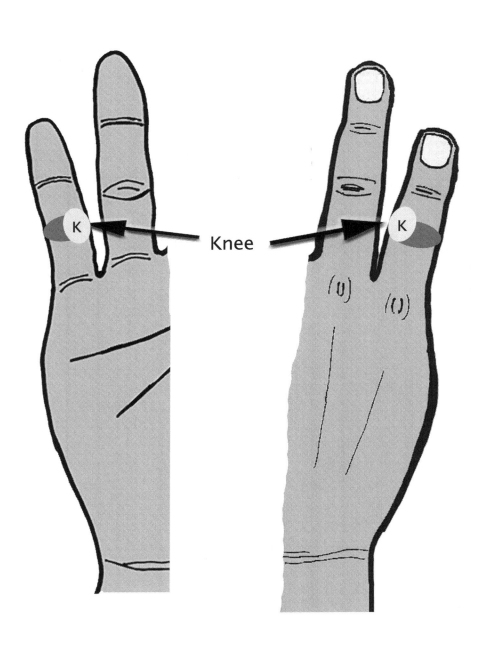

Knee

Knee Pain After a Fall

I was approached by one of the environmental services staff (which is the fancy term for the housekeeping department) when I arrived at one of the hospital nursing stations. She had seen me treat the nurses and asked if I could help her knee pain after a fall at work. She pointed to the brace on her right knee and said she took an over-the-counter pain medication before coming to work but her knee still hurt. She was thinking about going home because she was having trouble doing her job that day.

I found several tender points all around the second joint of her right pinky finger and stimulated them. She took the knee brace off and walked around the nursing station and did several knee bends, laughing in amazement at how much better her knee now felt. I advised her to apply pressure to the points I marked on her finger when the pain returns. She put the knee brace on top of her work cart and went right back to cleaning the patient rooms.

After I saw my patients, I left the hospital floor and returned a few hours later to see another patient. I asked the woman how her knee was doing. She showed me that she was wearing the knee brace on the other knee because her right knee felt fine but her left knee was now bothering her.

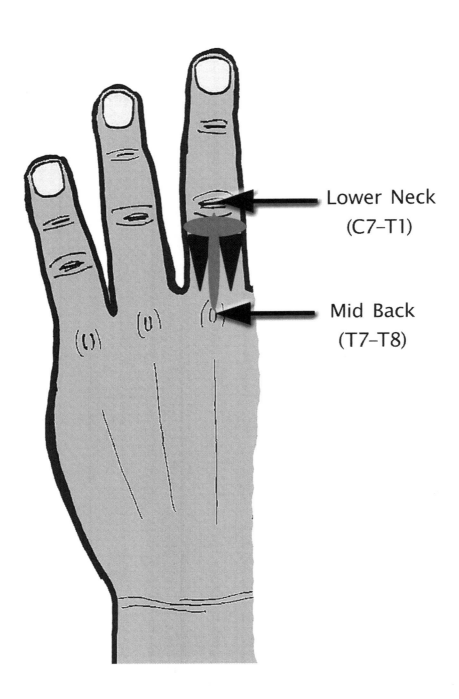

Lower Neck
(C7–T1)

Mid Back
(T7–T8)

Upper Back Pain

A woman who worked in the front office of my son's school stopped me one morning after I dropped him off at class. She knew I had treated my son's teachers and asked if I would help her too.

She had chronic muscle tension and pain above and between her shoulder blades which got worse each day from sitting in front a computer at work. I found several tender points on the back side of her middle finger, between the second and third joints. Most of the tender points were right below the second joint, corresponding to the area above the shoulder blades, and down the center of the finger, corresponding to the space between the shoulder blades. After marking the points and stimulating them, I asked her to move her arms and back to recheck the pain. She reported that the pain was much better and the muscles were less tense. She said it felt as if they had been loosened up after a massage. I told her to take a picture of the points on her hand and to stimulate those areas again with the tip of a pen when the pain returns.

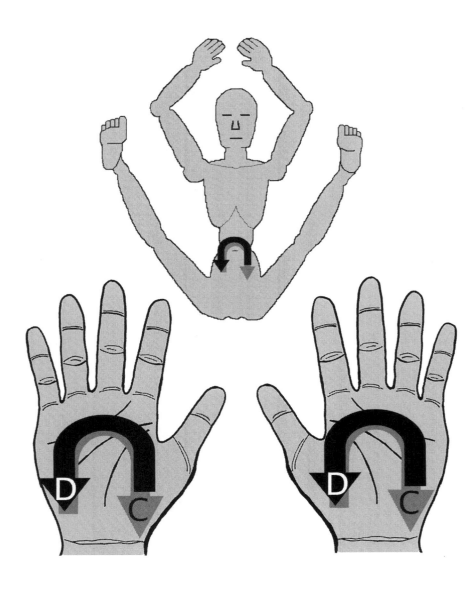

Diarrhea

One of the nurse practitioners came up to me at the hospital. When she leaned in towards me, I thought she was going to give me a hug. But instead she whispered in my ear, "I think I need to go home. I'm running to the bathroom with diarrhea every few minutes and can't get my work done."

I offered to show her where and how to rub her hand to slow down the diarrhea. At first she looked at me like I was crazy, but she said she would try anything at that point. I knew she was right-handed, so I held her left hand out in front of her with the palm facing outward. I explained that the normal movement of the colon is up the right side of the abdomen, across the area above the umbilicus, and down the left side. I then showed her the location of this same direction on her left hand. With her left hand held out in front of her body, the normal direction of movement of the bowels on her hands was clockwise, around the representation of the umbilicus in the center of the palm. Then I told her rubbing in that direction would be helpful in cases of constipation, to promote the normal movement of the intestines. For diarrhea, she needed to rub her palm in a counterclockwise direction, for the opposite effect to slow the movement of her bowels. I showed her how to do this using firm pressure with her thumb.

I saw her a few hours later and she reported that she had no additional episodes of diarrhea since she began rubbing her palm. She said others might think this was a coincidence and her condition had merely run its course, but she knew that she was not improving when she asked me for help.

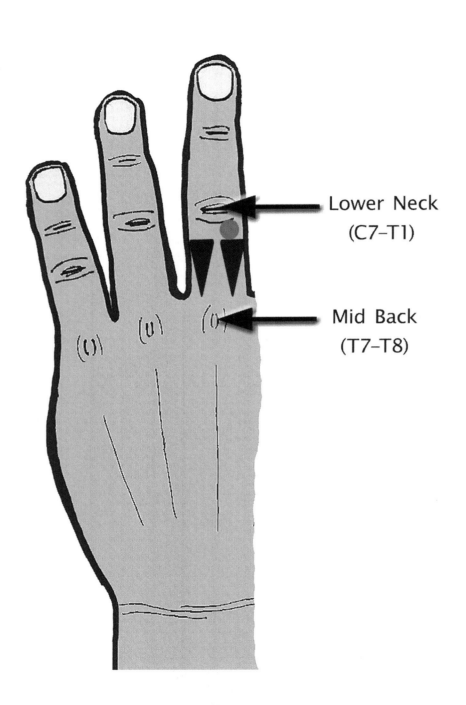

Lower Neck
(C7–T1)

Mid Back
(T7–T8)

Upper Back Pain Provoked by
Using the Computer

One of my son's teachers asked me to help her husband. He had an unusual problem - a discreet pain in his upper back, above the right shoulder blade when he had to use his computer mouse for long periods at work. The discomfort was enough to distract him from his work but the pain did not bother him at other times.

He repeated the movements he made with his right hand while using the computer mouse and could point with one finger to the precise location on his upper right back where he felt the pain. He was right-handed, so I used his left hand for treatment because the search area was on the middle finger. On the back of his left middle finger, I searched the area under the second joint that corresponds to the area above the right shoulder blade. I searched a large area on his finger and he told me that none of the points were tender. After a while, I found a single point that made him jump when I applied pressure with my probe and I marked it. I continued to search in the surrounding area for more tender points but found no more.

I stimulated the single point with brief pressure from my probe a few times and asked him to mimic the movement of his hand using the mouse again. Despite several minutes of trying to provoke the pain in his upper back, he was unsuccessful. He also said he felt the muscles in that part of his back were less tense. I told him to take a picture of the single mark on his hand so that he could quickly relieve his own pain whenever it returned.

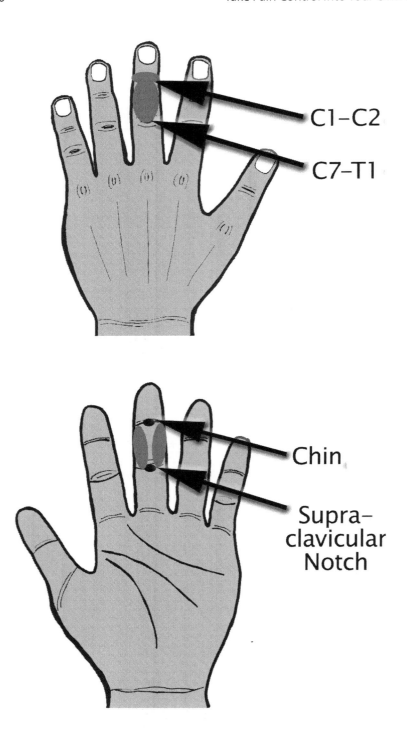

C1–C2

C7–T1

Chin

Supra-
clavicular
Notch

Chronic Neck Pain

While eating lunch with another doctor at the hospital, I mentioned that I was teaching a workshop at the University of Miami that weekend. She told me she had chronic neck pain and could not turn her head more than a few degrees to the left for years. She asked if I thought Korean Hand Therapy might help and I suggested we try it to find out. She tried turning her head to the left and had to stop almost immediately due to worsening pain in the back of her neck.

On the back side of her middle finger, between the first and second joints, every point I checked was tender. There were also lots of tender points at the first joint space and directly above it, representing the occiput. It took a while to activate all those points three times, and I used the roller on my probe to make sure I didn't miss any. I also used the roller on the palm side of the middle finger between the first two joints, because I suspected there were several tender points corresponding to the front of the neck as well.

I asked her to turn her head again. She grimaced in anticipation of the pain as she slowly turned her head to the left. To both of our surprise, she kept turning her head until her chin was directly over her left shoulder. "I can't believe it!" she exclaimed, as she repeated the movement over and over. "It's been years since I could do that and I didn't think what you did would actually work," she admitted. I told her to take a picture of the area on the back of her middle finger that was covered with dots from my marker. I told her to stimulate the points when the pain returns and I suggested she search the palm side of the middle finger with the tip of a ballpoint pen to find more points to treat.

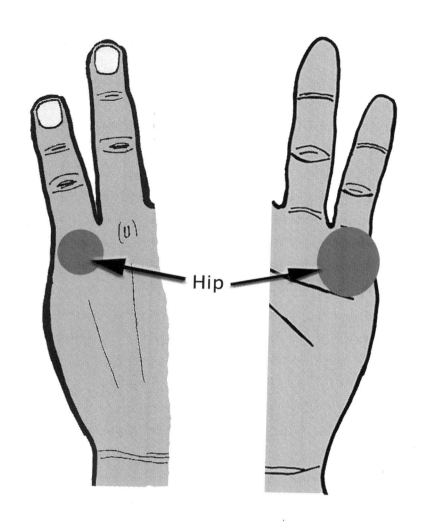

Hip

Hip Pain

I noticed a woman who works in the cafeteria was limping as she was pushing a cart of food into the doctor's dining room. This lady smiles all the time but that day she was not smiling and she grimaced briefly with almost every step. She told me that she needed a hip replacement because of bad arthritis. Her surgery was in two weeks and she could not stay home because she needed to save her sick days for recovery after surgery. She told me she could not take her prescription pain medication while at work because it made her tired and the over-the-counter medication didn't help much. Her left hip pain was especially bad that day, so it was a struggle to get her work done. I told her I could poke on her finger to give her some relief and she said she would try anything.

Using her left hand, I did an extensive search of the third joint of her pinky finger and found many tender points on the front and back of it. I stimulated the points and asked her to walk around to recheck how her left hip felt. She was surprised at how the pain was better so quickly and said when she walked she primarily noticed pain in her right hip, where she also had severe arthritis but not to the point where she needed surgery yet. I then searched for tender points on the third joint of her pinky finger on the right hand and stimulated them. She walked around to check the results and then smiled, laughed, and did a little dance. She looked at her hands in disbelief and told me she couldn't believe that just pressing on them reduced the pain. I told her to stimulate those areas again when the pain returns. She said she could not wait to return to the hospital cafeteria to tell her co-workers about what had happened.

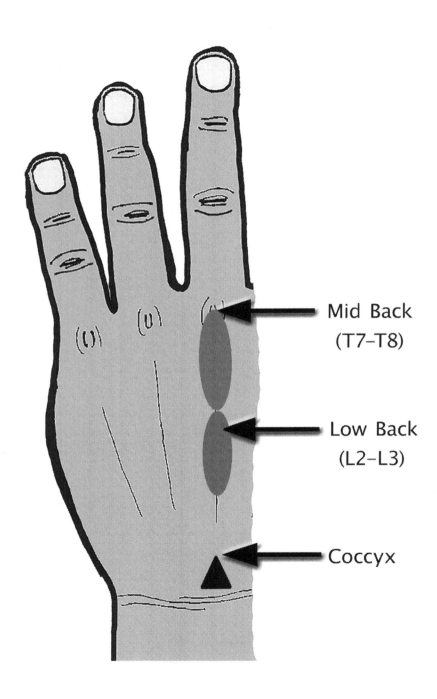

Mid Back
(T7–T8)

Low Back
(L2–L3)

Coccyx

Chronic Lumbar Back Pain

My son's teacher asked me to help her husband who had a long history of back pain. Her husband told me about all the things he had tried in the past without results and was surprised when I told him I did not need to know any of that before treating him. I asked him to point to his pain, and he pointed to the lumbo-sacral area of his back and showed me that he could only bend forward slightly before the pain stopped him.

I searched for painful points on the back of his hand, in the corresponding area, halfway between T7-T8 and the coccyx. He said none of the points were tender but many of them had dark purple discolorations, so I knew they were active. I told him that I wasn't looking for points that cause unbearable pain, just those that were those that were uncomfortable. When I rechecked the points, he said they were tender, so I marked and stimulated them.

At first, he reported no difference in his back pain. He did stretching exercises and I noticed that he could bend further forward than before, although he said he did not notice any difference. He reported his pain was now worse above the area he previously showed me. I checked his hand again and found tender points in the new area and more points that he had first reported as non-tender in the first area. After I stimulated all the points, he could bend further forward and declared that his back pain was better but was disappointed that it was not gone. I explained that, given his chronic back pain, no one would expect him to become pain free and some immediate relief was a good thing.

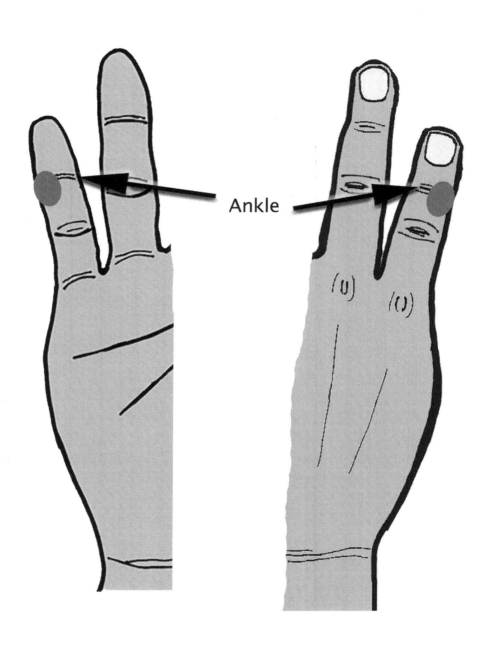

Ankle

Ankle Pain

I was in the doctor's dining room at one of the hospitals and overheard one of the surgeons talking on the phone nearby. He was complaining to a friend about his ankle pain that kept him from being able to exercise. When he hung up the phone, I asked him if he felt the ankle pain at that time and he said yes. I told him I did acupuncture and could do something to help him that didn't use any needles. He said he was willing to give it a try and rolled up his right pant leg and pulled down his sock. I explained that I was going to use his hand, not his ankle. He gave me a skeptical look, saying "My hands?" while holding them up to his face. I told him I realized that, as a surgeon, his hands were important to him, but I promised not to damage them and only really needed to use his pinky finger.

Before we began, I made him take a few steps across the room to confirm that the pain was indeed still there and so he could localize it more easily. The pain was on the outer part of his right ankle, so I checked the palm and back sides of his right pinky finger. At first, he was reluctant to say any of the points I checked on his finger were tender, but I eventually found several points that were more uncomfortable that others in the surrounding area. After stimulating the points, I asked him to walk around again. He was surprised that he could not find the pain anymore. I told him that if the pain returns he should stimulate on the points I had marked on his finger.

I saw him weeks later and he complained that the pain had returned. I asked him if he had pressed on the points again and he said no. I reminded him that even prescription pain medication wears off and that he should stimulate the tender points to get pain relief whenever the pain bothered him.

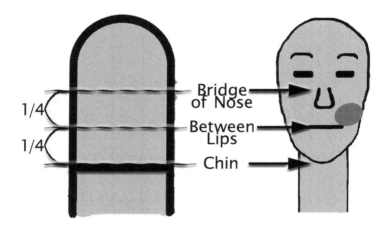

1/4

1/4

Bridge
of Nose

Between
Lips

Chin

Dental Pain From Extensive Dental Work

When I arrived at my son's preschool to pick him up, I could tell there was something wrong with his teacher. She looked miserable and had her hand pressed against her left jaw while chasing a room full of toddlers. I asked her what was wrong. She told me she was in the middle of a series of extensive dental procedures and the pain was horrible. Whenever she moved her mouth or bit down, the pain flared. Her dentist had given her prescription pain medication, but it made her sleepy so she could not take it while working.

I offered to help her with Korean Hand Therapy. My son, who had seen me treat some of his other teachers, encouraged her to let me do it. He gave her a long explanation about which finger was the head and which ones were the arms and legs. The teacher looked doubtful, but told me she was in so much pain that she would try anything. I asked her which hand she wrote with and she told me she was right-handed, so I used her left hand for treatment. Because the head, neck and trunk are represented on the middle finger, either hand can be used to treat pain in the center of the body.

There were several points that were extremely tender on the palm side of her middle fingertip, in the area corresponding to her upper left molars and jaw. I remember barely having to apply any pressure to them to determine that they were active points. For my own interest, I also checked the area where the upper right molars and jaw are located on the finger and found no tender points.

I stimulated the points I found and asked her to bite down gently and see if she noticed any difference. The look on her face was a combination of confusion and surprise, as she reported that the pain was much better. I held her left hand up with the palm facing forward and showed her that the points I had marked on the left side of the palm side of her middle fingertip represented the area on the left side of her upper jawbone and teeth where she had pain. I suggested she take a picture of the marked points on her finger to help her find the same area once the marks washed off.

Two days later, I asked the teacher how she was feeling and she told me her jaw was bothering her again. "How come you don't poke on your finger?" asked my son before I could say anything. She admitted that she had forgotten that she could help herself by stimulating the points on her finger. She picked up a pen, found the tender points on her middle fingertip again, and bit down to confirm that the pain in her jaw was better immediately. She gave my son a hug and said, "Next time you see that I'm having pain, please remind me to poke on my finger."

Resources

Take Pain Control Into Your Own Hands

- www.TakePainControl.com

Enlarged copies of handouts and color charts from this book,schedules of upcoming live and online workshops and monthly Q & A webinars, and a limited selection of probes and press pellets.

Korean Hand Therapy Supplies:

- www.khtsystems.com/KHT_Products.htm

(Dr Lobash has generously offered readers of this book a 10% discount on KHT products if you call to place an order and mention Take Pain Control Into Your Own Hands)

- www.MediKore.co.uk

Korean Hand Therapy Training:

- Dr. Dan Lobash:

www.easterncurrents.ca/learning/earn-ceus/recorded-courses/korean-hand-therapy

- Dr. Jong Baik:

www.JongBaik.co.uk

The Official Korean Hand Therapy Website:

- www.soojichim.com (a small section is in English)

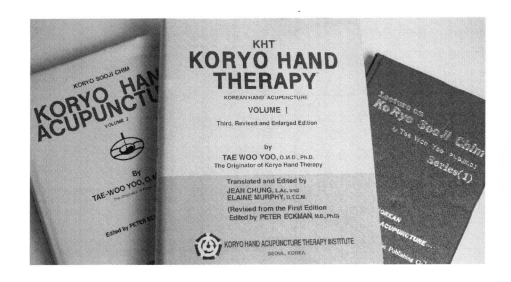

The Wu Project and Korean Hand Therapy

As you may have read on the back of this book, ten percent of the profits from this book are being donated to The Wu Project. Your purchase of this book will help medically underserved communities around the world learn Correspondence Korean Hand Therapy, along with other safe and effective treatment modalities.

The Wu Project, Inc., is a 501-c-3 not-for-profit organization, founded by Alicia Villamarin, PhD, AP, and Maria Rosa Romero, DVM, AP in 2014. These two energetic healers lead trips with volunteers to isolated communities in places like Nepal, Cuba, Guatemala and Mexico, teaching traditional Chinese healthcare practices to local healers in underserved communities.

I met Alicia and Maria in 2017 at a University of Miami conference and told them about the workshops I teach. They recognized the brilliant simplicity of Correspondence Korean Therapy and knew it would be a perfect modality to add to the curriculum they teach in remote regions around the world. Although both of them are experienced acupuncturists, they had never learned Korean Hand Therapy. I met with them soon afterward and went through the workshop training. They taught Correspondence Korean Hand Therapy for the first time in Chiapas, Mexico and will add it to the educational modules they are planning in other places

I could not stop smiling when I saw this photo of Maria and Alicia with their students in Mexico, proudly showing off points on their hands. The students quickly learned Correspondence Korean Hand Therapy and several had pain relieving results with it right away.

If this book helps you manage your pain, please consider supporting this worthy cause. Indigenous groups around the world have few options for treating pain due to poverty, political instability, and limited access to medication and doctors. Imagine the impact that Correspondence Korean Therapy would have if it became common knowledge in these isolated parts of the world. For more information, go to www.TheWuProject.com .

References

Boehler M, Mitterschiffthaler G, Schlager A. Korean hand acupressure reduces postoperative nausea and vomiting after gynecological laparoscopic surgery. Anesth Analg. 2002 Apr;94(4):872-875.

Hedegaard H, Warner M, Miniño AM. Drug overdose deaths in the United States, 1999–2016. NCHS Data Brief, no 294. Hyattsville, MD: National Center for Health Statistics. 2017/ CDC. Wide-ranging online data for epidemiologic research (WONDER). Atlanta, GA: CDC, National Center for Health Statistics; 2016. http://wonder.cdc.gov .

Institute of Medicine Report from the Committee on Advancing Pain Research, Care, and Education: Relieving Pain in America, A Blueprint for Transforming Prevention, Care, Education and Research. The National Academies Press, 2011. http://books.nap.edu/openbook.php?record_id=13172&page=1 .

Jodorkovsky R. Hand acupuncture experience in pediatric patients. Medical Acupuncture. 1999;11(1):25-28.

Jodorkovsky, R. Treatment of primary nocturnal enuresis with hand therapy: a randomized, double-blind, placebo-controlled trial. Medical Acupuncture, 2003, 14(2), 28-31.

Kim KS, et al. Capsicum plaster at the korean hand acupuncture point reduces postoperative nausea and vomiting after abdominal hysterectomy. Anesth Analg 2002, Oct;95(4):1103-1107.

Kobrin LE. Comprehensive Acupuncture Therapy Without Needles Medical Acupuncture. 2000 Spring/Summer;12(2):29-30.

Koo, MS, et al. Antiemetic efficacy of capsicum plaster on acupuncture points in patients undergoing thyroid operation. Korean J Anesthesiol. 2013 Dec; 65(6): 539-543.

Ochi JW. Korean hand therapy for tonsillectomy pain in children. Int J Pediatr Otorhinolaryngol. 2015 Aug; 79 (8):1263-1267.

Park HS, et al. Prevention of postoperative sore throat using capsicum plaster applied at the Korean hand acupuncture point. Anaesthesia 2004 Jul;59 (7): 647-651.

Park KH, Yoo T. Relieving Migraine Headache by Regulating Cerebral Blood Flow with Koryo Hand Therapy. The Internet Journal of Alternative Medicine. 2000 Volume 1 Number 1. http://ispub.com/IJAM/1/1/4345 .

Park KH, Yoo T. Useful Method To Confirm Tender Points Of Primary Headache: Corresponding Points Of Koryo Hand Acupuncture Therapy. The Internet Journal of Alternative Medicine. 2004 Volume 3 Number 1. http://ispub.com/ IJAM/3/1/6526 .

Park, KH, et al. Effect of Acupuncture on Blood Flow Velocity and Volume in Common Carotid and Vertebral Arteries in Migraine Patients. Medical Acupuncture, 2009, 21(1).

Penfield, W. & Boldrey, E. (1937). Somatic motor and sensory representation in the cerebral cortex of man as studied by electrical stimulation. Brain 60: 389-443.

Rudd RA, Seth P, David F, Scholl L. Increases in Drug and Opioid-Involved Overdose Deaths — United States, 2010–2015. MMWR Morb Mortal Wkly Rep. ePub: 16 December 2016. DOI: http://dx.doi.org/10.15585/mmwr. mm655051e1 .

Schlager A, Boehler M, Pühringer F. Korean hand acupressure reduces postoperative vomiting in children after strabismus surgery. Br J Anaesth. 2000 Aug;85(2):267-270.

Shin, HS et al. Effects of koryo hand therapy on serum hormones and menopausal symptoms in Korean women. Journal of Transcultural Nursing, 2010, 21(2), 134-142.

Stewart WF, Ricci JA, Chee E, Morganstein D. Lost productive work time costs from health conditions in the United States: results from the American Productivity Audit. J Occup Environ Med. 2003 Dec;45(12):1234-46.

Yoo, Tae-Woo. Koryo Sooji Chim: Koryo Hand Acupuncture, Volume 1, First Edition. Eum Yang Mek Jin Publishing Co., Seoul, Korea. 1988, pp 473.

Yoo, Tae-Woo. KHT Koryo Hand Therapy, Volume 1, Third Edition. Koryo Hand Acupuncture Therapy Institute, Seoul, Korea. 2011, pp 684.

Notes:

Made in the USA
San Bernardino, CA
25 February 2018